RESOURCES FOR EARLY LEARNING: Children, Adults and Stuff

RESOURCES FOR EARLY LEARNING:
Children, Adults and Stuff

PAT GURA

SERIES EDITOR TINA BRUCE

P·C·P
Paul Chapman
Publishing

ACKNOWLEDGEMENTS

I am grateful to the staff and children of Redford House Nursery, Roehampton Institute London and the Dorothy Gardner Nursery Centre, Westminster for allowing me to watch and photograph them in action and for me to use a selection of the photos in this book. Thank you also to Sue Wadhams for giving me permission to use her photographic sequence of the climbing frame, which appears in Chapter 2. The material on Froebels Gifts in Chapter 6 was put together with the help of Jane Read, The Early Childhood Archive, Froebel Institute College, Roehampton Institute London. As ever, thank you Jane.

Pat Gura, Sept. 96

Reprinted 2001

Paul Chapman Publishing Ltd
A SAGE Publications Company
6 Bonhill Street
London EC2A 4PU

SAGE Publications Inc
2455 Teller Road
Thousand Oaks, California 91320

SAGE Publications India Pvt Ltd
32, M-Block Market
Greater Kailash - I
New Delhi 110 048

British Library Cataloguing in Publication data
A catalogue record for this book is available from the British Library

ISBN 0 7619 7359 1

Library of Congress catalog card number

Reprinted for SAGE publications by the Alden Group, Oxford

British Library Cataloguing in Publication Data

Guru, Pat
    Resources for early learning. _ (0_8 years series)
    1. Resource progrfams (Education) 2. Education, Primary
    I. title
    372.1'3'078

First published 1996
Impression number   10   9   8   7   6   5   4   3   2   1
Year   2000   1999   1998   1997   1996

Typeset by Wearset, Boldon, Tyne and Wear.

CONTENTS

SERIES PREFACE – 0–8 YEARS

At most times in history and in most parts of the world, the first eight years of life have been seen as the first phase of living. Ideally, during this period, children learn who they are; about those who are significant to them; and how their world is. They learn to take part, and how to contribute creatively, imaginatively, sensitively and reflectively.

Children learn through and with the people they love and the people who care for them. They learn through being physically active, through real, direct experiences, and through learning how to make and use symbolic systems, such as play, language and representation. Whether children are at home, in nursery schools, classes, family centres, day nurseries, or playgroups (now re-named pre-schools), workplace nurseries, primary schools, they need informed adults who can help them. The series will help those who work with young children, in whatever capacity, to be as informed as possible about this first phase of living.

From the age of eight years all the developing and learning can be consolidated, hopefully in ways which build on what has gone before.

In this series, different books emphasise different aspects of the first phase of living. *Getting to Know You* and *Learning to be Strong* give high status to adults (parents and early-childhood specialists of all kinds) who love and work with children. *Getting to Know You*, by Lynne Bartholomew and Tina Bruce, focuses on the importance of adults in the lives of children. Observing children in spontaneous situations at Redford House Nursery (a workplace nursery) and in a variety of other settings, the book emulates the spirit of Susan Isaacs. This means using theory to interpret observations and recording the progress of children as they are supported and extended in their development and learning. The book is full of examples of good practice in record-keeping. Unless we know and understand our children, unless we act effectively on what we know, we cannot help them very much.

Learning to be Strong: Integrating Education and Care in Early Childhood, by Margy Whalley, helps us to see how important it is that all the adults living or working with children act as a team. This is undoubtedly one of the most important kinds of partnership that human beings ever make. When adults come together and use their energy in an orchestrated way on behalf of the child, then care and education become integrated. Pen Green Centre for Under-fives and Families is the story of the development of education with care which Margaret McMillan would have admired. Beacons of excellence continue to shine and illuminate practice through the ages, transcending the passing of time.

Just as the first two books emphasise the importance of the adult helping the child, the next two focus *on* the child. John Matthews helps us to focus on one of the ways in which children learn to use symbolic systems. In *Helping Children to Draw and Paint in Early Childhood*, he looks at how children keep hold of the experiences they have through the process of representation. Children's drawings and paintings are looked at in a way which goes beyond the superficial, and helps us to understand details. This means the adult can help the child better. Doing this is a complex process, but the book suggests ways which are easy to understand and is full of real examples.

In *Helping Children to Learn through a Movement Perspective*, Mollie Davies, an internationally respected movement expert with years of practical experience of working with young children, writes about the central place of movement within the learning process. In a lively, well-illustrated book, with lots of real examples, she makes a case for movement as a common denominator of the total development of children, and in this draws our attention to its integrating function. A whole chapter is devoted to dance – the art form of movement. The provision of a readily accessible movement framework gives excellent opportunities for adults to plan, observe and record their children's development in movement terms.

Self-Esteem and Successful Early Learning by Rosemary Roberts is about the importance of being positive, encouraging and gently firm in bringing up and working with young children. Whilst every family is different, every family shares some aspects of living with young children. These are taken up and given focus in the book in ways that are accessible and lead to practical strategies. The reader meets a variety of situations with the family and explores successful ways of tackling them so that the theories supporting the practice become meaningful and useful.

The Development of Language and Literacy by Marian Whitehead emphasises the importance of the people children meet, and the need for adults to be sensitive to the child's culture, feelings and developing ideas as conversations are made, and early attempts to communicate in writing and reading emerge. Children need to spend time with people who care about them, enjoy being with them, and support their language.

Resources for Early Learning: Children, Adults and Stuff looks at the materials given to children in early years settings and takes a critical look at the conventional wisdom and assumptions early years workers make about sand, water, paint, blocks, the home area, etc. This book encourages practitioners to be reflective about their practice.

Clinging to dogma, 'I believe children need . . .' or saying 'What was good enough for me . . .' is not good enough. Children deserve better than that. The pursuit of excellence means being informed. This series will help adults to increase their knowledge and understanding of the 'first phase of living', and to act in the light of this for the good of children.

TINA BRUCE

INTRODUCTION

There are certain play materials that you must provide, however limited the space and however difficult the circumstances.

(Roberts, 1971 p.9)

The materials rated as essential were: dry and wet sand, water, blocks, clay, paint and a home corner. There is, however, no explanation for this no-nonsense statement. Was Roberts simply passing on the 'conventional wisdom' which Bruner (1980, p.76) asserts has for several generations informed the resourcing and practices of early childhood education?

THE CRITICS

Bruner was commenting on the findings of a group of studies which he directed between 1974 and 1979 into aspects of the care and education of children under five. One of these studies, (Sylva et al., 1980), appeared to cast doubt on the power of materials, such as those mentioned by Roberts, to stretch children's thinking, stimulate their imagination or prolong concentration. Bruner observes (p.76):

One cannot resist the conclusion that far too little rational intelligence and informed research goes into early education.

Another piece of research (Hutt et al., 1989), also conducted during the late 1970s, found little to justify what it saw as the mandatory status of natural materials in the curriculum for under fives. These researchers wrote scathingly of statements made by early childhood educators, such as Yardley (1970) and Cass (1975), which seem to suggest a natural and sometimes mystical relationship between young children and materials like sand, clay, water and wood. From observations of children's personal, untutored encounters with clay, Yardley (op. cit. p.21) offers this impression:

A child . . . will pummel and knead, poke and flatten and hammer the material until the child and the material become one, and the visual results are the effects of experience shared. The child and the stuff in his (or her) hands embark on their exploration of one another.

Hutt et al. (op. cit. p.85) wondered whether such statements were more the 'picturesque products' of adult thinking than 'exact descriptions' of children's experiences with natural materials. Yardley's manner of describing children's experiences is discussed further in Chapter 2.

A PRACTITIONER'S TALE

Before moving from mainstream nursery education into alternative provision, I never questioned seriously the developing child's need for regular play with sand, water, clay, paints, blocks, nor their attractiveness to children. They were seen as part of Nature's Grand Design for young children who needed such materials for the healthy development of mind and body. Like vitamins, they worked in their mysterious and indispensable way. My job was to serve them up, on a daily basis.

It was only through practising in unfamiliar conditions, amongst colleagues whose experience and preparation for working with young children was often different from mine, that I began to question my assumptions about material provision.

A particularly formative period for me was as a pre-school playgroup course tutor in the early days of the playgroup movement. Statutory provision for under-fives has always fallen far short of demand. Since the 1960s, part-time, voluntary playgroups, run by groups of parents in their homes and church and community halls, have provided a significant proportion of group play facilities for three- to five-year-olds in the UK. Until Brenda Crowe was appointed as the first National Adviser to the Pre-school Playgroups Association (now the Pre-school Learning Alliance) in the early 1970s, preparation for work in playgroups was very patchy and often in the hands of nursery teachers like myself, taking time out from teaching to care for our own young children.

As playgroup course tutors some of us assumed, to begin with, that all we had to do was hand over the practices associated with 'good' nursery education, particularly ideas about play and materials, to playgroup supervisors and helpers.

On one evening per week for a term, we would pass on the Good News about water, sand and malleable materials, like clay and dough and so on. At the end of the course we would ask for comments and questions. Invariably participants would ask for more ideas of things to do with the children. Taken aback, we would ask: 'But what about water play, sand and dough?', only to be told: 'We've done them.'

Becoming self-critical

Seriously chastened, and with the help of Brenda Crowe, we learned that 'good practice' cannot simply be given away, just because it is good. Being good is not the same as being obvious. We became aware that it is not only young children who learn from experience. She helped us to think about what it is to 'learn', and about *ourselves* as lifelong learners.

As workers in the field of early childhood education, we all need opportunities to discover in our own time and on our own terms what the purpose and potential of different materials might be as resources for development and learning. As tutors, many of us needed time for learning as much as those we were supposed to be helping. Brenda enabled us to think about materials by encouraging us to explore and experiment for ourselves and to observe and *wonder* about what children did with the materials they were offered, in the way they were offered.

One of her particularly memorable suggestions was that instead of always providing rolling-pins, cutters and bun tins with the dough, we might try sometimes using just hands. We were encouraged to sit with the children and observe the effects of this change. We wondered whether anyone would want to participate, under these circumstances. Would they know what to do with the dough? Our more usual provision with the rolling-pins and other aids invariably suggested a familiar cooking routine to the children: first they rolled the dough, then cut it and placed the pieces one by one in the hollows of the bun tins. Many children know the sequence by heart, from having seen it performed at home. Others pick it up from them. To extend the experience, an adult might enquire about the number of buns made and engage the cook in some counting. Then, if allowed, the buns are taken to the home corner to be baked in the oven. This, of course, means that the dough is no longer available for anyone else to use, until someone retrieves it. In my experience this is often at clearing-up time. The whole process might last less than five minutes. Sometimes, however, a party ritual is added, especially when an adult is present and willing to play along.

There are many processes being rehearsed and refined in 'cooking'. Rolling out a piece of dough involves several co-ordinations: exerting just the right amount of downward pressure and distributing this evenly along the rolling-pin, whilst simultaneously employing a push–pull action and continuously adjusting all of this to the changing shape and size of the dough. Given the complexities, children learn to do this remarkably quickly. Again this may be due to experience at home. As a child, I can remember hovering around the kitchen table, whenever my mother did some baking, watching her closely, waiting for the magical moment when the trimmings dropped from the edges of the pie plate, under her knife. By tradition, these went to the children. When mum was finished we were allowed the use of the rolling-pin to make our own pie from the trimmings plus a few currants. Pie-trimmings is a tradition which I suspect has its variant in many households and cultures.

Painting can take many forms (see p. xvii)

When just hands were used, as Brenda had suggested, a vast range of alternative scenarios emerged, often influenced by the colour and consistency of the dough. Pastel coloured and puffy afforded different experiences to shiny, strongly coloured, firm-textured dough.

One child I observed spent over an hour trying to make a skipping rope from dough made with self-raising flour and water. This has a springy, marshmallow texture and is very resistant to shaping. It is ideal for making worms which stretch and shrink like real ones. Making a rope-like form with material which seems to have a life of its own requires a special technique which needs practice. Every so often the rope was given an experimental mid-air twirl. Then it was back to the drawing board for modification, before being tried again. Theories and suggestions abounded as to why it kept breaking: 'give it some handles', 'give it more dough', 'roll it more slowly', 'put a real rope inside it'. This last suggestion gave the ropemaker a wonderful idea. She gathered up her dough and, taking it over to the doormat, gently pressed it onto the surface. When lifted off, it was textured by the slender sea grass ropes from which the mat was made. 'Now it will work,' she said. It didn't, of course, but no matter – the making and testing continued.

Play? With clay?

A playgroup set up in a primary school specifically for Traveller children offered many opportunities for questioning the received wisdom about certain materials. The playgroup was seen as an informal and welcoming point of entry for Travellers wishing to bring their children into school whenever they were in the area. It was modelled on traditional nursery practice and provision and offered all the 'essentials'. Before long, we realised the children were not using the equipment in ways that we expected. The clay was never touched but we persevered in presenting it every day, believing that once tried, they would love it. They didn't 'play' with the water either, or the dressing-up clothes. Instead, they would take buckets from the sand tray, fill them at the water tray, then with kneeling mats and cloths improvised from dressing-up clothes, proceed to clean the floor, furniture and windows, *in earnest*. During their time with us, we did not see these children exploring or experimenting with water. It was not a plaything for Travellers. Not surprising when you think about it.

One day all the children's mothers stayed for the whole session. They had been having problems with local authority bailiffs who were trying to evict them from the land where they were encamped. They stayed because they were afraid of what might happen to the children, if they (the mothers) and their vans were towed away whilst the children were at playgroup.

On this particular day, in an effort to tempt the children into playing with clay, I took a large lump of the stuff and began pummelling, rolling, poking and shaping it, talking aloud about what I was doing. The children ignored my antics. Turning to their mothers to see if they could be persuaded to play, I noticed for the first time that they were all wearing wellingtons caked in the raw clay of their campsite. Some of the children were also affected. The rest had probably been carried from the encampment. In this moment of truth, I caught one mother's eye and we both started to laugh. That day, we all learned something new about clay.

If water and clay were not a huge success from our perspective, the home corner was no more so, modelled as it was on a suburban villa which stays in one place. The children dealt with it by loading the contents into prams and travelling off up the drive with them.

The interpretation *we* had given to the home corner and its trappings were not meaningful in the same way to this group of young children – as indeed it may not be for many children on first arrival in an early childhood setting. Yet we behave as if it were obvious and sometimes react to children who do not as if they have a problem. Outside the school setting, children make their own play homes, under the table, behind the settee, on the doorstep. In the autumn they sweep leaves into enclosures and patterns of rooms. Often we can see children trying to do something similar in school when they 'liberate' bits of *our* provision and set up home in the book corner, block area, bathroom, or outdoors in the bushes.

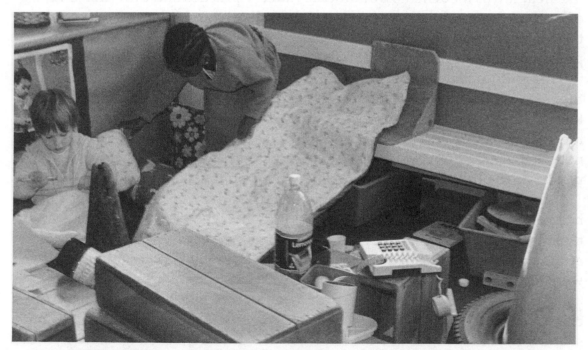

Impromptu play home

Fieldgames

The early childhood tradition is so fixated on 'corners' that in the pioneer days of the outdoor playparks known as One o'Clock Clubs, we even tried putting commercially designed home corner screens in the corners of fields. In these exposed positions they sometimes competed with galeforce winds to stay upright. At times like this we began to ask ourselves: *what really matters?*

From habit, old hands like myself persist in using the term 'corner' to refer to any designated space or area. However, to save confusion, I have dropped this in favour of 'area' throughout the rest of the book.

One o'Clock Clubs, introduced in the early 1960s by the Greater London Council, were originally intended to help bridge the gap between supply and demand for opportunities for young children to meet and do things together. The clubs were located in fenced-off areas of local parks. Entrance was free and it was conditional that carers stayed with their charges. Inevitably this meant that babies and toddlers attended alongside their three- to five-year-old siblings. The 0–5 age range meant that we were constantly needing to rethink our material provision, especially as everything happened in one big space.

Paint pots were a problem. Childproof lids are an excellent deterrent to paint drinkers and pourers but also to those who only want to see or stir the paint.

At first we could not imagine any form of painting which did not demand paper and easels or tables. The easels blew over unless tied to the wooden railings and the paper flapped about or blew away. Adapting means to ends and ends to means, the children invented railing painting. These were the railings which formed the boundary between the One o'Clock Club and the rest of the park. Children came with their carers from miles around to paint them in riotous colours and patterns which changed daily, and sometimes several times a day.

Paradoxically, considering the extent to which early childhood educators traditionally draw inspiration from the natural world, we seemed to lose sight of it completely when given a field to play in.

THE PRESENT BOOK

The emphasis in this Introduction has been on 'stuff' because it is in this direction that criticism has come from outside the profession. In this book, stuff is set in context with people and communities, where it has always been. Throughout the book the connections between children, adults and stuff are made more explicit than they have been in the past.

A change of job helps but is not essential in gaining a fresh perspective. Strategies to help us think through our practices are discussed throughout the book, using as a central frame of reference the principles discussed in Chapter 3.

These principles represent the underlying rationale of the book and draw on the work of Tina Bruce and other colleagues in early childhood education.

Throughout this Introduction I have reflected on research and events which have challenged my understandings and expectations and caused me to wonder about what I was doing and why. Refreshing ourselves does not necessarily result in change. Often it leads to confirmation and greater confidence in what we know and do. It can help us become more fully *aware* of and accountable in *professional* terms for what, how and why we engage in this practice or that.

1 STUFF

In this chapter the value of the term 'play material' is questioned. This is linked to a discussion of the role of 'stuff' in the education of the 'whole child'.

MATERIAL PROVISION

The term 'stuff' used in the title of this book is a form of shorthand referring loosely to a wide range of materials: natural materials, 'found' and recycled materials, mark-makers, climbing apparatus, books, toys, puzzles, games, electronic equipment, tools. It was deliberately chosen to avoid using the overworked and misleading term 'play material'. Early learning makes use of stuff in both play and work contexts. Arguably, there is no material, or substance, not even a toy which is by its nature a play material. Anything can *become* a play material, as the player wills it: a child's duffle-coat worn by its owner as a Batman cape is a play material *whilst play lasts*.

Structured play

Casual use of the term 'play material' to refer to all manner of stuff, regardless of how it is being used at any given moment, may be directly responsible for the bizarre adult notion of 'structured play'. This is the term used to refer to adult-initiated activities involving 'play materials' in pursuit of pre-determined learning outcomes. An example of this comes from the 1970s when the purpose of dolls in early years classrooms, from an adult perspective, seemed to be entirely to do with mathematics. Dolls were purchased in threes, each being a different height for size-ordering: short, taller, tallest. Each was provided with an appropriately sized bed and matching sets of clothing. The intention was that the right doll would be dressed in the right clothes and put into the right bed. In my experience this was a game mostly played by adults after the children had gone home, leaving the dolls stark naked.

Contrast this with a story told me by a mother. Whilst doing a bit of mending, she had paused to watch and listen to her four-year-old daughter who had borrowed the pincushion and was now making up a story using it as the stage. The dressmaker's pins sprouting from it became the actors and stage props. Three pins sized short, taller, tallest, became respectively the little girl,

Anything can 'become' a play material, as the player wills it (p.1)

her mum and dad. This well-ordered pin family went for a walk in the forest (tall pins) and picked bunches of flowers (glass-headed pins, grouped by colour).

Young children have their own criteria for judging the difference between play and work as we shall see in Chapter 9. They talk of enjoying the tasks adults set them at the sand or water tray but they see these as work not play. In referring to practical activities with materials as 'structured play' we are misled into thinking we have provided for play. If we were to call it 'work', which is how children experience it, there would be less risk of our overlooking the need to plan for play *in children's terms, where their purposes prevail*.

THE LANGUAGES OF LEARNING

The older children get the more they are expected to learn through the spoken and written word. They are taught through subjects such as mathematics, science, art, history, music, geography and technology. Each of these subjects is like a different language. It has its own forms of speech and terminology which distinguishes it from other subjects. Each represents a different way of looking at the world and making sense of it. The power of our thinking as human beings is multiplied if we can become fluent in these different languages.

These languages of later learning are not the languages of early childhood. The late Italian educator, Loris Malaguzzi (1995), who had a great love and respect for young children, was concerned that they should not be hurried into learning through separate subject matter. He urged parents and educators to allow and encourage young children to use and develop their understandings of the world through what he describes as the hundred or more 'languages' of early childhood. These include: movement, sound, paint and other mark-making and colouring materials, speech, print, games, construction materials, toys, puzzles, story and make-believe, clay, sand, water, space, light and most importantly with and through the medium of people. The development of the mind includes what we care about and what uplifts us as well as knowledge and understandings. It involves children in the use of their bodies as well as the brain. It involves seeing, hearing, scenting, tasting, touching. Through this multitude of languages young children view the world and try to make sense of what they see. In using the term 'languages' to describe the multi-media of early learning, Malaguzzi provides us with a metaphor which enables us to recognise that they work in the same way as the languages of later learning.

When young children are thrust prematurely into the languages of later learning, they are deprived of their own very powerful ways of building knowledge and understandings. In short, they are handicapped. This represents a great loss not only to children but to humanity. It is through children that adults can glimpse or rediscover those things which are hidden from eyes and ears conditioned to seeing and hearing only what they expect.

> *One of the most stunning horizontal creations made with blocks that I have ever come across was of a spider's web, the result of much keen observation and preliminary sketching on the part of a four-year-old. It spread across a vast expanse of floor and managed to convey the impression of both spider and web simultaneously. The remarkable similarity of form between a spider and its web had never before that moment occurred to me and the wonder of it was very moving. Through a child's eyes I was seeing something anew.*
>
> *(Gura, ed., 1992 p.128)*

The more young children know, understand and can do through immersing themselves in the stuff of the world with the people who share it with them, the more confident they become and the more they can get to know. This is because what any of us already know, understand and can do at any given moment, is the point at which we start when trying to make sense of new experiences. The narrower the range of early experience, the more fearful children are in the face of the new. However, wide-ranging experience without depth can be as ineffective in building confidence and supporting children's disposition to learn as too narrow a range. It is through the involvement of adults and older children, who have some idea of the possibilities of different kinds of stuff and greater all-round knowledge and know-how, that depth of experience is increased.

SUMMARY

The non-committal term 'stuff' was chosen as an alternative to the casual and sometimes misleading use of the term 'play material' to refer to the material provision of early learning. To convey something of the significance of the multi-media approach to early learning, a parallel was drawn between the languages of later learning and those of early childhood, using Malaguzzi's notion of the one hundred languages of children. In the next chapter, we look closely at children learning with their whole selves, using several of their languages on and through the climbing frame.

2 ON AND THROUGH THE CLIMBING FRAME

INTRODUCTION

Really good stuff for early learning serves the whole child by affording opportunities for a wide range of interconnected experience and learning. This chapter is based on a talk I gave some years ago to a group of nursery parents to illustrate this point. In the light of concerns expressed by some parents about whether children might be more gainfully employed in seat-based activities than in what they saw as less educational, more physical, outdoor activities, I chose the climbing frame as my example.

The climbing frame

Becoming a climber

The climbing frame is one of the most popular pieces of equipment in the nursery and some children base many of their activities on it. The obvious attraction is in terms of vigorous physical activity in which both girls and boys revel and which is so important for their developing bodies. Then there is the building of confidence which results from mastering the challenges and obstacles presented by the arrangement of steps, rungs, platforms and various add-ons. To climb safely, children have to concentrate hard on where they place their hands and feet and in what order. At the same time they must remember to watch out for the heads, hands and feet of other children. They discover that climbing up, although not easy for a beginner, is easier than coming down. Children's first thoughts about how to climb down seem to suggest to them that they should turn to face outward as if about to walk down a staircase. The reality is more like being on a sheer cliff face with your back to the mountain and can be very scary. The ground seems very far away. A child may feel panicky at this point and need to be talked through the idea of turning round and coming down backwards. It soon becomes apparent that these seemingly simple terms are anything but. Remember that what we are calling backwards was forwards on the way up. Once they are the right way round for the descent, the problem becomes one of not having eyes in their feet. Going up, the hands and eyes led the way, working together. Going down, feet and brain must communicate with each other, without the benefit of sight, through touch and the alternate shifting of first one hand and foot and then the other. Sometimes the reassuring presence of a trusted adult is all that is needed to ensure a safe descent for novice climbers. As they grow more confident, they discover the quick way down: they jump from the top. A well-judged jump from the climbing frame affords the thrill and satisfaction of take-off, flying and a safe landing. Before jumping, they learn to check what is going on below, so as not to land on anyone. They must also judge the angle at which to launch themselves and the amount of outward thrust needed in order to land safely on the mat.

Play begins

A meeting place

In addition to these more obvious uses, the climbing frame is an excellent place for meeting other children. It is the communal perch where several children may sit and watch the everyday life of nursery folk unfolding. As they observe, they may pass comments, give advice and gossip. They can learn a great deal about people in this way, for example how different adults and children behave in different situations. From watching how others tackle problems like wanting the same piece of equipment at the same time as someone else, they can begin to speculate on how others think and feel.

Collaboration and elaboration

Change of view

Standing atop the climbing frame, the child's head is some six or seven feet in the air. The world can be viewed from a steeper angle than usual and this makes everything look different. The extra height gives children a birds-eye view, enabling them to see both far and wide. People who are waist high or less to a 5'6 inch tall adult, normally see only bits of nearby objects, large animals and features of the landscape. The birds-eye view from the climbing frame enables them, perhaps for the first time, to become aware that the sandpit is square shaped and the nursery has a sloping roof like buildings in books. There is much for children to wonder about from their position above the ground. Over time, they piece together in their minds the view from the ground with that from above. We can get some idea of the differences these alternative viewpoints make by squatting down to the height of a young child and then standing on a chair, or by comparing the view from the ground floor of a building with that from the first floor.

Make-believe

Using their knowledge, understanding and imagination, and with the addition of a few props like a steering wheel, blankets, a tea-set and a telephone, children often pretend the climbing frame is a car, spaceship, bus, hospital, house. They learn to share and work out their ideas with other children through discovering that personal interests and satisfaction sometimes have to be sacrificed to keep a good group game going. Mild disagreements with others can lead to new learning about the world around, about self and others.

The importance of opportunities to imagine in the form of make-believe play for the development of children's minds cannot be over-stressed. Our imagination allows us to behave 'as if' something were so: like making believe the climbing frame is a house and is burning down, or a tennis ball in a plateful of sand is stew and dumplings. It allows us to put ourselves into the shoes of other people; to try to think how they might behave in this situation or that; to work out what they might be thinking and feeling.

As adults we indulge in make-believe when we watch a film. The power of our imagination is such that when we watch a film, we can experience genuine emotion, we can have an opinion about the events and the people we are watching, we may shout abuse or call out advice to them, even though we know they cannot

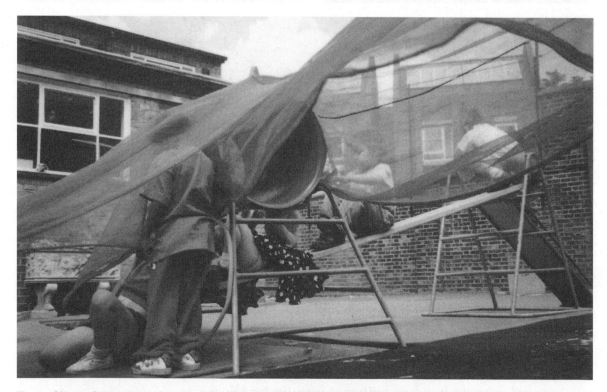

Turn taking and sequencing: 'up the slide, down the plank, through the hoop and round again'

hear us and we know 'it's only a story'. So it is for children engaged in make-believe.

These things which the imagination allows us to do amount to a phenomenal increase in our power to think, feel and act. They mean we can think about things which are not happening to us and are not immediately in front of us. We can consider the possible consequence of doing this or that before going into action. In other words, we can plan. When we listen to children engaged in make-believe play, we become aware of how much planning is involved. The imagination enables us to make intelligent guesses about the meaning of events and the behaviour of others; to question, solve problems, design, create and invent, to venture into the unknown with care. If we look and listen closely to children's make-believe play on and around the climbing frame and elsewhere, we can see and hear them practising all of these very important human life-skills.

A landmark
Some children use the climbing frame as a landmark which helps them keep their bearings. For others it is a point of arrival and departure, with games of chase and imaginary journeys beginning and ending there. It is a centrepoint, an island or planet around which children orbit on foot, or on wheeled vehicles.

Maximum gain
The climbing frame helps make it possible for all of these formative experiences to merge one into the other, thus allowing children to use their minds and bodies, their time and energy to maximum all-round effect.

Parent's responses

Access
This description of the climbing frame as a hub of physical, intellectual, emotional and social activity created a lively discussion between parents and staff. One parent said she was now worrying that her child might come home and say she *hadn't* 'played climbing'. Although this was said light-heartedly, it raises the important question of access and the possibility that amongst the children who do not make use of this or that, there may be those who would like to join in but for some reason are holding back. We need to make it our business to know not only *how* the material provision is being used but also *who* is and is not using particular categories of stuff.

Safety
Another area of concern for parents was safety. The staff reassured them that for reasons of safety and out of respect for the children's own wisdom in these

things, we neither coax them onto the climbing frame, nor to jump from it, even with a helping hand. The development of self-discipline, self-reliance and a concern for the safety of others as well as themselves, are far more important educational goals than the undeniable but momentary pleasure of being lifted up and jumped down by an adult. However, we would always help down a child who was in genuine distress.

We tread a delicate balance in providing equipment such as climbing frames between offering children freedom to adventure and the need to ensure their safety. For example, on two occasions, in different settings, I noticed small groups of boys aged three to five years climbing, in one case with ballpoint pens sticking out of their mouths and in the second, pencils. On each occasion they told me they were smoking cigarettes. My immediate reaction was for their physical safety and I persuaded them to hand over the pens and pencils.

- What lessons could we draw from this?

- Should the children be lectured about the dangers of smoking? – after all, it was only make-believe.

- What might be an appropriate response from a member of staff after noticing such a thing?

Another question of safety was:

- can we allow children safely onto the climbing frame wearing the dress-up clothes which are often part of make-believe play?

Summary

Sharing our ideas about learning in early childhood with members of children's families is not optional. It is part of our job. We need to listen to their concerns and make them our own. Sometimes this is just the kind of incentive, discussed in the Introduction, which we need in order to step back from our practice to try to see it from the outside, as a stranger might.

In preparing for this talk I became increasingly aware of the climbing frame, not only in its literal sense as a frame to climb *on* but also figuratively as a frame to climb *through*. Through the medium of the climbing frame children are enabled to see the physical and social world in new ways and to re-work their understandings.

In the talk, an attempt was made to describe and explain children's all-round activity on a single piece of equipment – the climbing frame. The result was not an exact description of what children were doing on any particular day, but rather an impression gained from watching the children closely on a daily basis, over a period of several weeks, plus a lifetime.

In discussing make-believe play, reference was made to its contribution to the development of children's ability to put themselves into the shoes of others and try to see things as they might. In this talk, I tried to put myself into the children's shoes. Perhaps this was the intention of writers mentioned in the Introduction to this book, such as Alice Yardley, whose descriptions of children interacting with all manner of stuff gave such offence to the researchers of the 1980s. Everyone who regularly engages with young children both in and out of the home must use both close observation *and* imagination to try to understand and communicate to others how the children they know well might be experiencing the world. Imagining, theorising and understanding are very close cousins. They are all essential in some measure in choosing, using and evaluating provision for early learning. In the next chapter we look at the beliefs and values which lie beneath the practices of early childhood education.

3 MATTERS OF PRINCIPLE

INTRODUCTION

The last chapter began with a reference to 'really good stuff' for early learning. Behind that 'really good' are ideas and ideals about which early childhood educators including myself care deeply. In this chapter, I will try to explain the values which guide my judgement in deciding what is 'really good stuff' for early learning.

Good and bad, as a neighbour of ours used to say, is 'all according', meaning it depends where you start. In education, the same practice from one viewpoint can be seen as good and from another as bad. Not long ago, several Members of Parliament called for closer inspection and monitoring of nursery education, with a view to bringing this into line with traditional whole-class teaching methods. According to one MP, nurseries put too great an emphasis on 'discovery methods'. Another stated: 'We are worried about the level of education they (i.e. nurseries) provide. They shouldn't just be about play.' (Hackett, 1991). From these comments it is possible to unravel the speakers' views of good and bad practice:

- **Good:** the 'giving' of pre-selected knowledge and skills to young children through whole-class teaching

- **Bad:** young children learning through their own efforts and interests, sometimes through the medium of play

By reversing the good/bad labels we gain the opposite view, the one which early childhood educators are accused of by these MPs.

Throughout this book, early childhood education is seen as embracing the years 0–8. Educational policies and practice relating to this age range are affected by at least two overlapping and sometimes conflicting approaches representing two different value systems: the *developmental* and the *academic*. The MPs referred to were advocates for the academic approach and the nursery practices they complain of could be described as developmental. In the next section, our need to be aware of where we stand is examined.

FACING UP TO OURSELVES

In the report of the Plowden Committee (CACE, 1967) into primary education in the 1960s, it was noted that even those primary school teachers regarded as the most gifted had difficulty in explaining to observers the basis of their practice. When someone asks: 'What made you think of doing that with the children?' and we reply by saying something like: 'I just knew in my bones the children would leap at it', we may be right, but we have given nothing away, not even to ourselves. Anyone wishing to learn from us will pick up only the surface features of what we do and soon find that is not enough. In the Introduction we saw how the difficulties experienced by tutors in communicating the notion of 'good practice' were the result not of the failure of playgroup leaders to get the message, but of tutors like myself not having grasped it themselves.

During the past decade, there has been a conscious effort to uncover the underlying guiding principles of the developmental approach to early childhood education (Blenkin and Kelly, 1987; Bruce, 1987).

By searching through writings on early childhood education from the late nineteenth and early twentieth centuries to the present day, Tina Bruce (ibid.) identified a cluster of basic principles which have guided successive generations of early childhood educators in planning, resourcing, implementing and evaluating the curriculum.

These principles provide some answers to *why* we do *what* we do in the *way* that we do it. Give or take minor differences in emphasis, they have been broadly recognised as representing a system of interrelated values or beliefs about a range of concerns. These are summarised below.

Concerns of the developmental approach

• human minds and human potential • the individual in society • young children • education • motivation • freedom and control • the structuring of knowledge • cultures • learning processes • human relationships

---

Drawing on this body of work on principles of practice, we turn in the next section to a more detailed review of the characteristics which help define the developmental approach. All the concerns listed previously are interrelated and this is only partially reflected in the following section.

THE DEVELOPMENTAL APPROACH

1 Human minds and human potential: the individual in society

From a developmental perspective *people* as individuals and members of cultural and social groupings are the core concern: what they are like *now* and what, in human terms, they are capable of becoming. This involves some notion of what it is to be fully human. The Brazilian teacher–philosopher Paulo Freire (1974) suggests we are only fully human when, with others, we are able to reflect on our lives and change them for the better. He saw language and literacy as the key to reflection, using these terms to include a whole range of symbolic languages, like art, poetry, music and drama. The work of Malaguzzi, described in Chapter 1, is about enabling young children to be fully human through their 'hundred languages'.

Being fully human might also include a sense of belonging, of being able to contribute something of oneself, to communicate with others, to make meaningful relationships. These are among the aims of New Zealand early childhood educators and endorsed by their government (Carr and May, 1993).

2 Young children

Young children are seen as vulnerable, impressionable and dependent, therefore early childhood education is concerned with all aspects of their well-being (Blenkin, 1995). This is sometimes expressed as a concern for the 'whole child'. An impression of what is meant by this might be gained by visualising a spider's web.

Parts and wholes

A spider's web is made up of the most delicate threads, yet it is strong enough to survive fierce winds and heavy rain. It gains its strength from the way in which the parts relate to each other to form a whole. The threads which radiate from the centrepoint are interlocked with those which encircle it, resulting in the strong and completely unified system of threads called a web. Drawing on the imagery of the spider's web, the 'whole child' can be visualised as a strong, web-like system of interrelated parts. The radial threads represent the physical, intellectual, emotional and social dimensions of the whole. The interlocking, encircling threads represent personal, cultural and social identity; moral, spiritual and aesthetic awareness.

As with the spider's web, it is the relationship *between the parts to the whole which make up the strong* functioning-whole *we call a child.*
(Web metaphor adapted from the model presented by Hazareesingh et al., 1989)

When we plan for learning in terms of separate dimensions of the whole we undermine the strength of the whole. In saying we are concerned about the whole child, we acknowledge that whatever we plan, provide or do, the effect is on the child as a whole. This was demonstrated in the last chapter and is seen repeatedly throughout this book.

3 Education

Education is seen as an open-ended, lifelong process. It is realised through active participation in the life of the world from day one. For example, we learn to speak our first language because we live in a community of speakers and listeners.

Language

At first our immediate and extended families induct us into the speaking and listening world by speaking and listening to us, by noting our interest in the objects and affairs of the world and helping us name and understand them through conversation, rhymes, songs and stories. A baby's earliest vocalisations are responded to as if they made sense. Speech develops in the context of two-way human relationships and experience in the speaking world, (Wells, 1987; Whitehead, 1990, 1996).

Reading, writing and number

Learning to read, write and use the number system begins in much the same way as learning to speak: by doing as others around are doing on a voluntary and informal basis and having all efforts treated seriously, as if they had meaning. Later learning builds on these intuitive beginnings (Gifford, 1995; Whitehead, ibid.).

4 Motivation: freedom and control

Young children are seen as natural self-starters, motivated by interest, curiosity and the desire to make sense of their world. They are keen to understand how to do things for themselves and to take increasing control of their lives. Parents confirm this when they say that their children: 'have minds of their own', 'are very determined', 'are always up to something', 'are into everything', 'never stop talking, even when they are asleep', 'always asking why this and why that', 'have vivid imaginations'.

Materials
the use of materials is not prescribed by adults but planned for on the basis of children's observed interests, developing knowledge and know-how.

The will to learn
Compulsion and formality are seen as removing control of the learning situation from children, with consequent effects on their will to learn. In later childhood, children can benefit from more formal approaches, but only if they emerge from early childhood with their will to learn undiminished.

Self-control
A central aim of this approach is the development of inner controls, that is, self-discipline. This is addressed in detail in the next chapter.

5 The structuring of knowledge; culture; learning processes

The division of knowledge into separate subjects is seen as only one of the possible ways of structuring what we know. It is not the way of all cultures, nor of people going about their everyday business. In the everyday world, knowledge is continually mixed and matched to suit different purposes. The usefulness of dividing knowledge into separate subjects is to do with the culture of secondary schools and universities and not apparent to young children. The learning of separate subjects can be seen as later extensions of early learning but not as replacements for it.

Internal structures
Early learning is believed to be structured by basic mental frameworks or schema (Piaget, 1951). These frameworks exist to kickstart the learning process by providing newborns with expectations which enable them to relate to the world outside their own mind and body from day one. Schema are patterns of distinguishing features such as movement, shape, form and sound. Babies are born ready to pick out these patterns from all the other sensations which surround them. Learning develops as a result of attempting to match patterns from the world outside to the schema inside our heads. As our outer world expands so our schema become more elaborated and vice versa. The more elaborated our schema, the more complex the connections we can make between areas of experience (1). (See also Chapter 8, p.55.)

Studying a single topic in depth

External structures

Social events help provide the external structures of early learning: hospital visits, a trip to the cinema, to the seaside; more regular events like mealtimes, going shopping, being read to and told stories, watching favourite television programmes. Rituals like toilet–hands–teeth–bed–story and the Happy Birthday song are also among the personally meaningful ingredients which give structure to children's lives and learning (Bretherton, 1984; Nelson, 1986).

In the spaces between events, children explore the physical world, sometimes alone, sometimes in the company of other children and adults. This may be done in the form of a topic or project, where something of general interest like a pond or a tree in the school grounds is studied in depth, beginning with the children's own impressions (Edwards et al., 1995; Katz and Chard, 1989).

Schema, events, books, stories, routines, rituals and topics, all help create a base from which children are able to consider new experiences.

Play

In play, children mix and match their knowledge, trying out new combinations of social and physical-world knowledge and practical know-how. Playing with what they know helps them to *think* about what they know and to gain confidence in using it.

Materials

Materials are seen not only as interesting in themselves, but as contributing to the 'languages' with which children represent and rework their knowledge, understandings, thoughts, wishes, beliefs, intentions and feelings.

Learning

This takes place as the result of the learner's desire to make sense of something puzzling, which does not match expectations. For this to happen, the learner must already have some ideas about the something in question.

> *When two three-year-olds decided to turn the hole they were digging into a paddling pool, they were intrigued when the two buckets of water they tipped into it had disappeared by the time they returned to add more. A paddling pool to them was a water-holding hollow. They had the hollow but not the water-holding and this became the challenge which lasted the entire afternoon. Their theories were wide-ranging and complex, particularly the one which involved the rate at which the water disappeared from the hole and the speed with which they could make a trip to the tap and back. If the latter could overtake the former, they theorised, their pool would stay full.*

Assessment

Regular and systematic observation enables appropriate opportunities for further experience and learning to be planned. (Blenkin and Kelly, 1992; Bartholomew and Bruce, 1993; Drummond, 1993).

The observations made by an adult, of the children trying to make a paddling pool, were used to help them bring closer together their emerging understandings of the problem and a possible solution. In school, it could have become the focus for a communal project.

6 Human relationships

Learning is done with and through other people. Children and adults are seen as partners in learning, with adults using their mature judgment about when to lead, to play an equal part, to follow or to stand back.

Parents

Parents and other family members and professionals are also seen as partners, sharing each other's wisdom and concerns for the whole child.

Research

The developmental position is supported by research findings in the fields of education, language and linguistics, developmental psychology and sociology (see Blenkin and Kelly, 1987 and Bruce, 1987). It also depends on enquiry-based practice for its effectiveness. This is discussed in Chapters 10 and 11.

SUMMARY

The concerns of this book are rooted in the system of beliefs just described. The developmental approach is sometimes caricatured as having little concern for knowledge and skill. This is complete nonsense. Knowledge is the basis of our expectations. If we expect nothing we can know nothing. The purpose of schema is to kickstart the knowledge building process. As children enter school the key questions about knowledge and skill become: which knowledge, which skills, at what time for what purposes. For the answers, we have to return to our starting point, our belief system.

The terms 'good' and 'bad' in this context are loaded with meaning. When referring to 'good stuff' for early learning, I mean materials which I and others who share the same beliefs can make use of to address the concerns of early childhood education from a developmental position. It is important to bear this in mind when seeking advice about what stuff to provide. We need to be wary of catalogue descriptions, recommendations and guidelines which do not make clear what they mean by 'good' and 'bad'. In the next chapter we look at stuff like water, earth, sand and clay in the context of children's developing understandings of the physical world, themselves and others.

Note

(1) For further reading on schema, see Athey, 1990; Bartholomew and Bruce, 1993; Davies, 1995; Matthews, 1994; Nutbrown, 1994; Roberts, 1995; Whalley, 1994.

4 Thinking And Feeling, Feeling And Thinking

Introduction

According to some sources, one advantage of materials like clay, sand, water and wood is that they can safely absorb the effects of being vigorously bashed, poked, pinched and sloshed. In making such materials available to young children, adults indicate that they accept the legitimacy of the strong, often negative feelings which are part of developing and learning. They also know that materials of this kind enable children to use their strong feelings creatively and constructively. Feelings are not simply discharged into materials but used to *transform* them.

Priorities of nursery workers

A deep concern for the emotional and mental well-being of young children seems to be a characteristic of people who choose to work professionally with them. According to Katz (1971) it may be a necessary condition. It infuses the writing of early childhood educators. An example from the early 1940s is in the characterisation of early childhood education as 'mothering' by Gwendolen Chesters (1943). By this she meant 'caring' of the kind which involves warmth, compassion and a commitment to each child as a unique person. She believed that the education of young children should be approached with care and understanding of the struggle involved in getting to grips with the complexities of being human. She wrote of the need young children have for a break from being 'little and inferior'; from trying to be good; from the conflicting feelings of love and hate surrounding close relationships and of anger and frustration in the face of difficulty. For a young child, coming to terms with the birth of a sibling was regarded as particularly fraught – and often is, where children feel themselves to be in competition for the attention of a carer. The conflict can be heard in three-year-old Lucy's question: 'If we put Baby Mark into a trouser press, would he turn into a picture of a baby?' It would be the perfect solution: allowing the new baby to stay, but in manageable form.

The need for 'space'

Chesters (ibid.) advised that children should get their break from coping through activities like hammering nails into wood and fists into clay, painting and drawing, make-believe, sand and water play, constructing and deconstructing with blocks. This was not an appeal for children to be allowed to escape from the world temporarily but of their right to 'space' in which to experience being in control.

Concern for the mental and emotional well-being of children is often taken to mean that early childhood educators are *less* concerned with the development of children's intellect. Is there a real dilemma here for early childhood educators or does it exist only in the minds of researchers and policymakers?

Research on aims and priorities

Attempts to discover what nursery workers believe to be the aims of nursery education have been frustrated by research methods which ask practitioners to choose between aims to do with thinking (intellectual) and those to do with feeling and relationships (emotional and social). When questioned in this way, aims to do with feelings and relationships have been placed first, with those to do with thinking coming second (Taylor et al., 1972). To check whether these results accurately reflected the views of practitioners, Audrey Curtis (1986) changed the rules to allow equal ranking of aims for those unable to choose *between* them. Thinking, feelings and relationships came joint first.

To avoid the pitfalls of this earlier research Linda Pound (1985) encouraged participants to describe their aims and priorities in their own terms. In this study, thinking, feelings and relationships were seen to be inseparable and to influence each other continuously. In order to further their intellectual development, practitioners believed the children needed to feel secure and confident in themselves in the nursery setting. Such feelings *critically* involve relationships with others. Poor relationships affect children's sense of safety and belonging and opportunities for learning with and through others. It was therefore seen as a priority to support children in forming relationships.

Making friends

The support we offer depends in part on our recognition that physical objects, apparatus and materials provide important sources of social contact between young children and between children and adults. They offer a common currency and provide shared reference points.

The points made by the teachers in Pound's study are vividly illustrated by a teacher–researcher, Vivian Paley in her book about Jason, a child who remains for a long time on the fringes of his peer group. He copes by immersing himself in a helicopter fantasy. He is pilot, engineer and plane, all rolled into one: 'Ask him a question,' writes Paley (1990, p.24), and he says his helicopter is broken. Suggest an activity and he rushes away to fix his helicopter.' His fantasy is treated with the utmost seriousness and respect by adults and children alike. Slowly and often painfully for all concerned, relationships are forged which make it possible for Jason to participate more fully in the life of his group. Paley demonstrates how every member of the group learned and developed in their thinking and feeling through these shared experiences. Above all, her work reminds us that the relationship between feeling and thinking, thinking and feeling make professional involvement in children's learning a deeply moral endeavour.

THEORY AND PRACTICE

The concerns of early childhood educators relating to the effects of mental and emotional processes on behaviour and states of mind, can be traced back to the psychodynamic theories of Freud. As a psychologist, Freud was concerned with disturbed adults. He developed a diagnostic process which enabled him, in effect, to unravel the adult mind back to early childhood and infancy. Through studying the case histories of his patients, he concluded that the origins of disturbance centred around unresolved anxieties arising in infancy and early childhood about the self and others.

Theories developed in clinics and laboratories seldom have anything direct to say to practitioners in any field and this is certainly true in the case of Freud relative to the teaching of young children. His concerns were with the diagnosis and healing of disturbed adults. The implications for early childhood education were worked out by educators like Susan Isaacs (1930; 1933) in terms of positive and supportive approaches to the inevitable anxieties of early childhood experienced by all children. These were seen as stemming from young children's awareness of their *dependency* on and need for others, coupled with a desire for *independence*. Our individual sense of personhood develops in the area between the two.

Through her writings, Isaacs legitimises physically vigorous, often messy activities. She suggests that children can satisfy both their emotional and intellectual needs simultaneously, through their engagement with each other and the physical world. As children become immersed in problem-solving with their materials, their attention is directed out towards the world rather than in on themselves, thus helping to extend and deepen their understandings of their relationship to the world and widen their horizons. In gaining increasing control of materials like sand and water through exploration and experimentation, they gain increasing control of themselves.

Controlling materials, controlling the self

Engaging the whole child

Lowenfeld (1935), like Isaacs, emphasised the complexity of children's use of materials. She suggested that when we describe play in terms of *separate* needs, such as emotional, intellectual, social, physical and spiritual, we risk over-simplification in our evaluation of both the materials and children's activities with them.

Her writing about play and the use of materials was based on her work with children presenting long-term behavioural problems, often to do with bladder or bowel control. Unlike Isaacs, the purpose of her work was diagnostic and remedial rather than educational. The materials in her playroom were based on her observations of what children select when free to play with what is to hand outdoors: water, earth, sand, wood and modelling materials.

Despite their present problems, Lowenfeld indicates how 'diverse strands of experience' become integrated in the play of her child-patients (p.16). She describes an episode involving a four-year-old who experimented for an hour with quantities of sand and water in a large bowl. The child alternately varied the proportions of sand to water. Sometimes the sand was submerged beneath the water, at other times sand and water merged into a single soggy mass. The child observed the effects she created until, to her evident delight, she arrived at the point where the amount of sand was sufficient to soak up all the water and leave a dry, lighter coloured layer above the darker, wet sand. Setting aside any clinical interpretations, Lowenfeld draws our attention to the way in which the child moved (pp.146–7):

> *perfectly logically from step to step, assimilating each step as it goes, and building carefully and concretely the following step upon the logical deductions of the first as is done in all forms of careful and logical thought.*

This episode of play vividly illustrates a constant theme of this book: the child as a functioning whole.

Play therapy

In this section, we take a closer look at play therapy, the context in which the above episode with sand and water occurred. It makes *clinical* use of materials like paint, sand, water, clay, earth, blocks, dolls and so on, for diagnostic and remedial purposes. It is an adaptation of the 'talking' processes Freud used with his adult patients, through which they reveal themselves. The distinction between the educational and clinical uses of sand, water, paint and clay has sometimes been blurred by misinterpretation of the writings of Susan Isaacs and her followers.

In my own preparation for working with young children in educational settings, great emphasis was placed on the therapeutic, or healing, qualities of the materials featured in this chapter. We worried about bottled-up feelings and the risk to children's mental health of frustrating their need to express them freely in the sand and water. We refrained from making suggestions about the use of materials lest we divert the children from their own more important purposes. We neither commented on nor asked about their paintings and drawings. Anything produced as a result of activity was believed to be of only passing interest to the child whose concern was only in the doing. Whilst not wanting to *under*-emphasise concern for children's emotional and mental well-being, I believe the hands-off approach has been *over*-stated in the past, leaving behind a legacy of uncertainty in the minds of many practitioners about boundaries, freedom and control.

The concerns we took upon ourselves and the methods we employed were based too closely on those of the play therapist. The purpose of play therapy is to try to uncover and remedy the causes of stress in young children, who are referred for this special approach. It is conducted under special circumstances, usually on a one-to-one basis by a qualified psychologist/play therapist.

'Wet, wet, water'

The classic example of play therapy in action is *Dibs In Search of Self* (Axeline, 1971). This is an account of a young child whose sense of personhood has been so damaged he denies his own existence. With the help of Axeline, his psychologist/play therapist, he finally 'finds' himself. Although the story of Dibs makes compulsive reading and is recommended to all who care for and about young children, this is a *clinical* case study and not a guide to the general use of play materials *outside the play therapy situation*.

Axeline neither approves nor disapproves when Dibs calculatedly and gleefully causes the water flowing from the tap to spray the playroom. Her technique is tailored to this child and their developing relationship. Reading on, we begin to understand that Dib's actions with the tap might be something to do with the testing of limits. Once again, he is playing at the sink, which is rapidly filling with water. he excitedly predicts that the water will 'be like a waterfall. It'll overflow.' He splashes some on his face (pp.128–9):

> *'Oh wet, wet water, so cool, so fast,' he said. He bent over until his face touched the water. Just as the water started to overflow, he quickly turned off the tap.*

Why does he stop at the last minute, on this occasion? Axeline, by her non-judgmental responses has enabled him to see that he is in control. He has the know-how to flood the playroom, *or not*, as *he* chooses. He is responsible for his own actions. Turning off the tap was the climax to a frenzy of unconstrained flinging and splashing of water.

Max and Dibs

There is a striking similarity between this episode with the water and the 'wild rumpus' orchestrated by the fictional Max in Sendak's story for children, *Where the Wild Things Are* (Sendak, 1970). Like Max, in effect, Dibs first unleashes his 'wild things', then he tames them. The crucial difference between Max and Dibs is that the rumpuses which Dibs orchestrates *actually take place*. For the fictional Max, it all happens in an imaginary dreamworld, when he is temporarily banished to his room by his mother.

In the everyday course of events, temporarily upset children will cope like Max, through their pretend play, in which they may incorporate sand, water, clay, paints, markers, dressing-up clothes, blocks, miniatures, dolls. Paley writes (1990 p.4):

> *Children are born knowing how to put every thought and feeling into story form. If they worry about being lost, they become the parents who search; if angry, they find a hot hippopotamus to impose his will on the world.*

Alternatively, they can reflect on their own experiences and feelings through stories like *Where the Wild Things Are*, rather than letting rip with the water like Dibs, when they need to affirm that they can create either order or chaos as they choose. This is because they will have been cared for in an atmosphere which values both freedom and control and is basically fair and reasonable in setting limits. An unco-operative Max had his freedom curtailed for a brief period by a loving but temporarily angry parent. Normal relations were very soon restored.

Children themselves understand the need for rules and develop a keen awareness of what is 'fair'. Observers have noted that when playing together, they spend as much time agreeing the rules of play as they do in actually playing.

Boundaries

These comparisons between the regular use of materials in early childhood settings and their specialised use in play therapy, will, I hope, help workers in everyday early years settings appreciate the important differences between them, especially in terms of boundaries. In everyday settings, children need guidance in reflecting not only on what has *already* happened but on the *possible* consequences of their actions *before* they take place. Often children do not know beforehand what effect their behaviour will have on themselves, other people, other creatures and inanimate objects and substances. Often there will be no opportunity for us, together with the children, to anticipate consequences reflectively, since we cannot be everywhere at once. For these reasons both fairness and firmness are needed in dealing with behaviour which strays over the limits. The bottom line is that behaviour likely to cause personal injury, or gratuitous distress of any kind to others, or damage to properly must be sanctioned. The setting of limits is discussed more fully in later chapters, with reference to the use of materials and social interaction.

SUMMARY

In this chapter the reasoning of early childhood educators in determining their priorities for young children has been explored. The study by Pound (1985) using nursery worker's own descriptions rather than outside researchers to frame their priorities suggests a way forward for research. The need for *children's* realities to form the basis of our descriptions stands out from the accounts of children in this chapter.

Materials such as sand, earth, water, clay and stones can stand up to vigorous handling by young children and cater for their changing moods and needs. Learning to control materials was linked to controlling the self and a distinction was made between the use of similar materials in everyday settings and the specialist practice of play therapy. Despite critical differences between the two situations, we saw that children in the therapy situation approach the materials with their whole, functioning selves, as they do everywhere.

The need for fair and reasonable rules relating to the use of materials was flagged for further discussion. Despite an apparent lack of rules, a careful reading of *Dibs* reveals the *patterning* of behaviour between the adult and child which becomes increasingly regular and predictable. However, the message of *Dibs*, for me, is more to do with the human spirit than with technique or materials. It is a celebration of the whole child. In the next chapter, we take a closer look at the business of choosing materials for early learning.

5 Choosing Stuff For Early Learning

Introduction

The original idea for this chapter was to offer a list of characteristics of 'good' stuff from a developmental perspective, to be used as a guide to acquiring or making stuff for early learning. This project has been abandoned and now the purpose of the chapter is to try to explain why.

How rather than what

After several decades spent working in the field of early childhood education I have become increasingly aware that choosing stuff for learning is considerably less problematic than using and subsequently evaluating it. It would be a simple matter for me to offer my top ten recommendations. The reason for not doing so is that materials do not work *for* us, we each have to learn to work *with* them, in what we believe to be the best interests of the children.

Among the candidates on my abandoned list of characteristics of good stuff were:

1   allows for the fluent, flexible way in which children engage with the environment
2   allows for originality and the elaboration of ideas

Fluency, flexibility, originality and elaboration have been identified as four characteristics of creativity (Torrance, 1970, cited by Edwards and Nabors, 1993, p.79). In my view, they typify young children's approach to life and learning – but they do not immediately make me think of wooden beads. The following observation was made by nursery nurse, Sharon Russell (personal communication).

Playing with beads

The curriculum plan was for a 'mathematics' activity involving the sorting and matching of beads according to size and colour. The provision for this was a bucket of assorted wooden beads, plastic bowls and squares of coloured card for sorting the beads into and onto. The intentions of the adult were explained to the four children who gathered around this presentation, after which they were left to direct the activity for themselves. The average age was 4.7 years. They used the materials as intended for about five minutes until, with the smoothest of gear shifts, Esra distributed the bowls, one to each child, then began filling them with assorted beads, explaining that she was giving them breakfast. Lee objected:

Lee: But they're beads.

Esra: No. You are the babies and I'm the mummy and I'm giving you
            breakfast.

Lee: Am I the dad?

Esra: O.K.

Yoke-Yin and Lee argue about the amount of food in their bowls:

Lee: I've got more than you.

Gemma: You have to share, count them so you have the same.

Lee: I don't want the same. I want more.

Yoke-Yin: I'm not playing then.

Lee: All right. I'll give you some.

Play continues along these lines, with each of the children contributing to the shaping of the action and dialogue. Eventually, breakfast is superseded by the 'cooking' of pizzas and burgers for a party. The storage bucket for the beads becomes the microwave and for several minutes the talk is about pizzas. Without announcement, Yoke-Yin begins to sort the beads by colour into the different bowls. Going with this, the others do likewise. The bowls now contain either red, blue, green or yellow beads and when the sorting is finished, each child claims one of the bowls. Nobody wants blue. Gemma, the peacemaker, eventually volunteers to have the blue:

Lee: That's silly. Pizza isn't blue.

Yoke-Yin: It doesn't matter. It's only pretend.

Esra: Anyway, I'm full up now.

Gemma: I'm going to wash up.

The beads, which have now become the 'dishes' are thrown into the storage bucket which is no longer a microwave but a sink.

What the children did with the beads fulfilled all four of the creativity criteria: it was flexible, fluid, original and continually elaborated on. From the stuff provided, the children created their own opportunities for all-round learning. However, this was not due to the stuff itself but to the possibilities this collection of objects suggested to that particular group of children at that moment. It is worth noting that in attending to their own important purposes, the children's activity included practical mathematics as part of the whole, rather than as an isolated activity, as first presented. This is intended as a moral tale, not as a plug for beads.

Beads, as such, are not creative materials. They are what we and the children see in them. The adult saw maths, the children saw food and food-related events. Nobody saw threading.

Creativity: parcel ribbon becomes 'Spiderman' thread when attached to wrists

In this episode, we saw children learning through the structures and processes described in Chapter 3. Through the re-enactment of a social event, they mix and match their understandings, trying out new combinations of social and physical world knowledge as well as more abstract notions like sharing and sameness; the idea of counting as a way of checking for sameness; ideas like more, less, like and not like.

The incidental coaching of Lee in the conventions of make-believe itself, are absorbed into the game. As he begins to feel more secure about make-believe, he falls in enthusiastically, with the idea of washing up. With continued help from his friends, he will soon be as accomplished at make-believe as Esra and Yoke-Yin and this will give him increased access to other minds, scenarios and stories. Given that make-believe is one of the most important 'languages' through which children communicate with each other and through which we can learn to communicate with them using storytelling, Lee can be seen to be on the verge of a most important breakthrough.

In the light of this episode, it seems that statements **1** and **2** may be a better guide to our *approach* than to our selection of stuff. It is *we* who must allow for children's creative approach to living and learning. The stuff itself knows nothing of creativity.

Setting limits

This is not, however, a recommendation that children should be allowed to do any old thing with any old thing, as the spirit moves. It is not in the best interests of children or the stuff we provide if, for example, we allow pieces of jigsaw puzzle to be used as fish and chips in the home area. This is because there are so many alternatives for pretend fish and chips but no alternative to puzzle pieces for someone who is trying to complete a puzzle. There is much that children can learn from having this pointed out to them. The question of boundaries and rules is the subject of Chapter 6.

ATTRACTIVE AND ENGAGING STUFF

Two particularly problematic characteristics which appeared on my abandoned list of materials were:

3   the power to attract children's attention
4   the power to engage children's minds

The one does not necessarily follow the other. As characteristics they may reside in quite different materials. Everyone who lives or works with young children will testify to embarrassing quantities of under-used stuff that has lost or never had any lasting appeal, or stuff that didn't 'take' as expected. We need to discover what attracts children to stuff initially and also how to help maintain and deepen their interest beyond the novelty stage. What causes their indifference to and avoidance of stuff? Strategies for exploring these questions are offered in Chapter 10. The remainder of this chapter will be used to examine two major reasons for some materials not taking off: familiarity and unfamiliarity.

NOVICES

Research repeatedly suggests that a three-year-old newcomer to the playgroup or nursery may spend the best part of his or her first two terms on the fringes of activity, watching others (Blatchford et al., 1982). The play with beads described earlier was closely watched by a much younger child who took over from the older children after they had finished. She seemed from her actions to be going over what she remembered from the earlier food play. Whilst it is true that children learn a great deal from watching others, we need to consider whether more direct adult support and input is needed to ensure that children get the most out of their early learning opportunities.

The 'settling in' of new entrants to playgroup, nursery and reception class settings is often concerned with relieving anxiety about separating from a loved one and abandonment to strangers. We may be less aware of anxiety arising from uncertainty about how to behave in this unfamiliar environment. This might persist long after separation anxiety has been overcome.

Fish in and out of water

The culture of early childhood education to people who are immersed in it, is like water to fish. It is their natural environment. They don't 'know' what it is they are in.

As a trainee nursery-nurse, I can remember the embarrassment of being told, kindly but firmly, on a fairly regular basis: 'We don't do that, dear.' They said it to the children as well. Their way of life was so impenetrable, it almost defeated me. Only when I confessed to feeling like a fish out of water did the headteacher realise she was a fish in it.

We need to think of new children as fish out of water, watching all the other fish swimming around and wondering how they do it. Swimming alongside a bigger fish could help.

RECYCLING THE FAMILIAR

In any new environment we look for the familiar. This is the secure base from which we extend our learning as well as our feelings about ourselves. For young children entering the nursery, playgroup or reception class, the familiar helps diminish the shock of the new. We need to ensure that they do not remain trapped in the familiar at the expense of broadening their base of interests and understandings. Taken to its extreme, children could emerge from their nursery, playgroup or reception class experience, without having ventured from the familiar into the unknown.

A little supported daring

We used to play a game in the nursery unit called 'Who's coming into the spooky old shed?'. Hamming it up, adults and children, hand-in-hand, would creep into the outdoor storage shed, close the door, cling to each other, shudder a bit and watch and wait for the return of our sight as our eyes got used to the dark. Then together we would shout: 'I can see!' It was one of those slightly dotty games people play together because it feels good. The story is offered here as a reminder that a little supported daring may be needed, if children are to learn to see beyond the here and now.

SUMMARY

The fate of stuff we have so carefully chosen with reference to our values and aims cannot be guaranteed when offered to children. Not because theory is a poor starting point but because we may expect too much from the materials as such, and are not putting enough of ourselves into closing the gap between theory and practice. In the next chapter we look at strategies for achieving this.

6 FREEDOM AND CONTROL I: SETTING LIMITS

INTRODUCTION

A central concern of the developmental approach is the development of inner controls, that is, self-discipline. As suggested in the previous chapter, this should not be interpreted as the right of children to do any old thing with any old thing and learn from their mistakes. The world they enter is an ongoing enterprise with rules and conventions already in place about:

- what people are free to decide for themselves

- what is merely advised

- what is negotiable

- what is definitely not on

It is also understood that, paradoxically, a rule can help set us free to relate to aspects of the world in new ways. These are the topics to be addressed in this chapter.

DEGREES OF FREEDOM AND CONTROL

In Chapter 4 we considered the relationship between the development of children's inner controls and strengths and their success or otherwise in dealing with the physical and social worlds. It was suggested that the inner and outer worlds of the child are one, acting in harmony with each other. If this is the case, we owe it to children to offer them opportunities to experience and come to terms with *degrees* of freedom and control. Ignoring absolute freedom and absolute control, which surely spell extinction in either direction, it is possible for us to reflect a range of degrees of freedom and control in our provision. At one end of the scale we need materials for using flexibly; at the other, a selection of puzzle-type stuff, which imposes its own rigid structure on a take-it-or-leave-it basis. Bridging these two positions, a range of stuff including tools, kits, sets of equipment and games is needed, where the degrees of freedom and control relating to their use needs careful negotiation and re-negotiation according to circumstances. We do not buy equipment on the basis of these criteria alone, of course, but we do need to maintain some kind of balance if we are serious about the development of self-discipline.

In the remainder of the chapter, a study of children's blockplay (Gura (ed) 1992, directed by Tina Bruce), is used to illustrate the power of rules to liberate. A description of the material and an excursion into history are necessary aspects of the story.

Blocks

Portrayed in the photograph below are large hollow blocks which can be used by children for building dens and 'vehicles' to fit with their make-believe play themes. A second type, portrayed on page 36, are unit blocks and these were the main focus of the research which was carried out by the Froebel Blockplay Research Group (1987–92) of which I was a member.

Large hollow blocks

Unit blocks

Froebel

A forerunner of the unit blocks on this page were the 'Gifts', shown on p.40, designed by educator–philosopher Friederich Froebel in the late nineteenth century. The scale was very small and they were meant for individual table-top use.

Froebel intended that the blocks he designed should be used to create:

- expressive designs – patterns and abstract forms

- representations of everyday objects, like chairs, beds, tables and architectural forms like houses, churches and bridges

- representations of mathematical shapes and forms using the surfaces, angles, shapes and forms of the blocks.

His methods for using blocks were rather formal by today's standards. The creation of the various forms was first demonstrated to the children by an adult.

An important part of the induction process concerned the removal of the blocks from their box, which was carefully turned upside down, lifted clear of the blocks and set to one side, like making a sandpie. The idea was that the child should experience the set as a *unified whole* before going on to an examination of the separate parts. At the end of the session, the separate blocks were reconstructed into a single cube. Members of the research group were introduced to Froebel's work as a matter of interest. At the time, his approach seemed to have little to offer.

From non-constructional to constructional uses

An initial review of the state of blockplay in participating groups revealed a tendency for the blocks to be used as any old stuff. By the end of the first twelve months, and without resorting to the prior instruction which Froebel believed to be necessary, some of the children were creating patterns, architectural and mathematical shapes and forms.

In dismissing Froebel's approach initially, we had failed to see that within it was the key to the 'language' of blocks. This was the rule that:

- Blocks must be seen and understood as parts of a whole set and not as a collection of parts.

Froebel knew how important it was for children to appreciate this in order for them to learn to use blocks to 'say' things with. If we want children to add the language of blocks to the languages of speech, movement, drawing and painting as part of their expressive and representational repertoire, we must first grasp the parts-of-a-whole rule of blockplay for ourselves. Then, through our own understanding, we must help children become increasingly aware of it. If you have access to a set of unit blocks, you might try the following activities which are aimed at raising awareness of the potential of a set of blocks. The activities were not designed for young children. If you can do this with a partner, so much the better. Have paper and pencil handy to record the arrangements you make.

Blockplay for adults

- Take two quarter units (3.5 × 7 × 14 cm approx) and see how many *distinctly* different ways you can find to put them together (the record, I believe, is 40).
- Now take four quarter units and repeat as above. (Most people are surprised at what can be done with so few blocks.) Now that you are getting the feel of the material:
    - use the whole set to make the story of the three bears;
    - use the whole set to make a 3-dimensional architectural form or decorative sculpture which is hollow inside. (One group used this particular challenge to try to build a pyramid and very nearly succeeded.)

If you have been able to get some hands-on experience with the blocks yourself, you will have realised that every block in a set is a potential partner to every other block. This means they need to be presented in such a way that children can see the whole range of shapes and sizes and be able to mix and match them to achieve their expressive and representational purposes. Children need opportunities to get to know every block and the basic combinations which can be made with them in order to acquire fluency in their use. They will do this without instruction provided they have an *intact* set of blocks to explore and not bits and pieces.

Basic rules

Two basic rules are needed if children are to be free to learn the language of blocks:

- Blocks stay in the block area.

- There should be a place for every block and every block in its place.

The block area
The block area may not be a permanent fixture. It is wherever the blocks are based when they are in use. An effective and easy way of indicating the boundary beyond which constructions must not spread nor blocks stray is to outline an area of the floor with masking tape.

A place for every block

Ways need to be devised for displaying blocks so the children can make choices. When it is time to clear the blocks away, each block should be returned to its own place. Many people use cut-out shapes pasted on shelves; others use special storage chests. Grocery boxes will do with pasted-on outlines to indicate which blocks they contain.

Collaboration

Adults and children need to collaborate in creating the conditions for blockplay to develop and thrive in. Children appreciate being asked their advice about such problems as boundaries and storage and have a vested interest in seeing that rules they helped to make are kept. The two basic rules on p.38 are the foundation on which a system of rules aimed at supporting the children in their blockplay can be created. One group made a rule which stated:

*   You must not take down a construction which has been left standing without asking permission of the builder.

Some days all the blocks are used by the children who are first into the block area. It is often very conflicting for them to dismantle what they have just created, in order that other children can have a turn. We made sketches and took photos, but this is not always possible or even desirable. It became accepted in this particular group that provided no-one else needed the blocks immediately, a construction could be left standing and only dismantled with permission. Built into the rule was the understanding that the builder had the right to give *or* refuse permission. Given the choice, they were invariably generous.

SUMMARY

Children's inner controls are strengthened when they are given the opportunity to think about their actions through genuine choices and genuine responsibilities presented through various kinds of material provision. The potential of rules to create possibilities which would otherwise remain undiscovered was illustrated with reference to research on children's blockplay. Of course, there is much more to blockplay than rules. What has been highlighted here is what seem to be essential preconditions.

In the next chapter, the theme of freedom and control continues. We look at a rule imposed by a teacher who it saw as non-negotiable. It was nevertheless intended as a liberation strategy and relates to the social dimension of early learning.

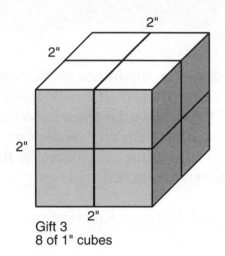

Gift 3
8 of 1" cubes

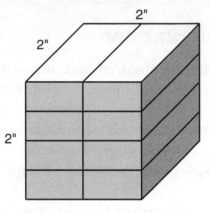

Gift 4
8 of 1" x ½" x 2" oblong blocks

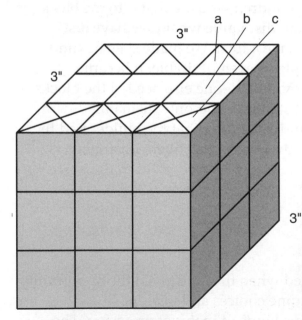

Gift 5 (cut from 27 cubes)
a) 6 of ½" cube cut diagonally
b) 21 of 1" cube
c) 12 of ¼ cube cut diagonally

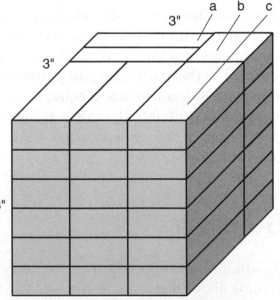

Gift 6 (cut from 27 oblong blocks)
a) 6 of 2" x ½" x ½" oblong columns
b) 12 of 1" x 1" x ½" square blocks
c) 18 of 1" x ½" x 2" oblong blocks

Froebel's Gifts 3, 4, 5 and 6

7 FREEDOM AND CONTROL II: THE INDIVIDUAL AND THE GROUP

INTRODUCTION

Children and adults who come together to learn are 'members of a group', not a collection of individuals. Each member affects every other member directly or indirectly, knowingly or unknowingly. In this chapter we look at 'the group' as a system of human relationships and, in particular, at the moral responsibilities of group membership.

THE 'AMIABLE CIRCLE': BELONGING AND CONTRIBUTING

In Chapter 3 it was suggested that dimensions of humanness might include a sense of belonging, of having something to contribute, and relationships with others. Each of these dimensions is embedded in the idea of an 'amiable circle' of change and development, described by Alison Stallibrass (1974) who ran a playgroup in her own home in the 1960s.

When children play *alone* at home with the same materials as those offered in a playgroup or nursery, the subsequent learning is entirely dependent on the input of a single mind interacting with materials. Stallibrass compares this to the group setting where each unique individual interacts *with others* in the shared material environment. Change and development occurs in both individual and group terms as children interact with each other at the same time as interacting with materials. The materials also change and develop in the sense that new individual and group learning is continually applied to them. This continuous extending of children, which in turn extends the material, which further extends the children, is what Stallibrass meant by the 'amiable circle' of development.

The give and take which keeps the amiable circle in motion, creates a sense of belonging and community. The lone child, by comparison, is stuck in an intellectual and social cul-de-sac.

Interaction

In order to sustain the amiable circle of change and development, we need to ensure that all the people who make up the group can connect with each other and the whole group. Extended periods of time are needed when members can interact freely. Space, furniture, seating, the presentation of activities need to be organised so as to allow freedom of movement and the pooling of minds which leads to the development of ideas. Play, games, stories, conversation and discussion provide key social contexts through which the amiable circle is constantly refuelled.

THE VICIOUS CIRCLE: REJECTION AND EXCLUSION

In such a set-up, how much freedom should children have to choose with whom they will interact? What if there are children who are excluded from the freely chosen activities of others?

Young children discriminate against different groups just as adults do on the basis of skin colour, physique, gender and other perceived differences. Individual children may be excluded because they smell permanently of urine, or have gained a reputation for not sharing, not playing by the rules, being bossy, clumsy or rough. Excluding behaviour is often the result of the conservatism described in Chapter 5, which propels us towards the familiar. Avoiding and ignoring behaviours exclude just as much as more openly hostile forms.

The younger they are, the less children are aware of the cumulative effects on another person, of being excluded from the company of others, and of the possible lifelong consequences: the rejected begin to reject themselves and may become alienated from the mainstream. In the early years, when children begin rejecting others, they are not thinking that far ahead.

In human terms, excluding behaviour is as bad for the development of the excluder as for the excluded. In contrast to the amiable circle, the rejection of group members can be seen as creating a 'vicious circle' of development for all.

The emergent racism and gender stereotyping which we see in young children and their perceptions of physical attractiveness and normality reflect the values of the wider society. Increasingly, early childhood educators are trying to find ways to break the vicious circle, to halt the perpetual recycling of discrimination, by creating opportunities for children to think about their fellow humans in new ways.

Breaking the vicious circle

One day, after much reflection, the early childhood educator Vivian Paley decided that it was no longer possible for her to stand back from children's excluding behaviours on the grounds that five- and six-year-old children were too young to understand. She reasoned that by the time children *are* able to understand, it is too late for those they have hurt. She decided to become the conscience of the group and made up a rule: 'You can't say you can't play' (Paley, 1992).

The children were given several weeks in which to get used to this new idea before it came into operation. During these weeks they had the opportunity to express and discuss their views as a group. As her contribution to the debate, Paley shuttled between year groups across the whole early childhood age range in her school, putting the rule to each group, in turn. First she would tell each group what the previous group had thought about it, then she would ask for their opinion. In this way all opinions were fed forward to the next group, until the last group was reached. The oldest children she consulted urged her to recommend the rule to the youngest children, those in the nursery, before it was too late. Some of these older children could remember rejecting others, some remembered being rejected, some carried the scars. Having canvassed the views of the early childhood population across the school, Paley returned to each group to report back what she had learned from the other groups. In this way the older children were able to ponder the thoughts of the younger and vice-versa, with each gaining new insights on themselves and others. Through her shuttle diplomacy she created a dialogue where there had been none, which continued after the rule came into effect.

When the day finally came, the rule was written out and posted around the room, to remind everyone. It could now be invoked by any member of the group by reference, not to the teacher, but to one of these notices. The rule gave all the children the opportunity to work on their relationships.

During a recent visit to Roehampton Institute, London, Vivian Paley was asked by Margy Whalley, Head of Pen Green Centre for Under Fives and Their Families, where such a rule would leave children who wished to play alone. She was thinking of children like Rosie, one of a family of five children, whose only hope of time and space to herself was at the Centre. Vivian Paley agreed with Margy that Rosie's right to solitude should be protected.

Paley also described how the implications of implementing the rule had begun to reveal themselves after its launch. For example, for many years it has been her practice to gather the group together each day to watch and perhaps take part in the dramatisation of stories made up by members of the group. Prior to the new rule, the author of a story could choose who was to act in it. They usually chose on the basis of friendship, which resulted in some children never being *freely* chosen. This seemed contrary to the spirit of the new rule, says Paley, so it had to go and was replaced with a rota system. By this means everyone was guaranteed the chance, in turn, to be in someone else's story. It is possible to imagine many other contexts where free choice of partner would no longer be tenable under such a rule: in games, dancing, physical education.

PROFESSIONAL DECISION-MAKING

There is much for us to reflect on in this story of the introduction of a rule. Sometimes we tread a very fine line when we put individual rights in the balance. Which individual and which rights should have priority? The individual who always chooses to play with person A rather than person B – or with person B who always gets left out? Professional decision-making involves reference to our principles. If our aim is the creation of amiable circles of change and development which acknowledge the relatedness of individuals to others, then we have to weigh in against any rights *assumed* by members of the group at the expense of others.

The introduction of the rule was made on moral grounds because Paley knew the children could not yet be reached through moral argument. The rule was intended as a support to enable them to reach higher moral ground. It was a mechanism designed to help them enter into each other's lives through reflective discussion, personal stories and play. There are enormous implications in terms of supporting children in the keeping of such a rule.

SUPPORT STRATEGIES

If it becomes unlawful in the group to discriminate against anyone on any grounds, the immediate problem shifts from that of access, to the help which can be given to the child who smells permanently of urine, the clumsy and those who don't yet know how to play with others, or are still a bit in the dark about make-believe.

The child who smells of urine, or has any other problem related to personal hygiene, needs our professional help and loving care. To give it, we may need to seek the advice of the family health visitor. At all costs the self-respect of the family and the child must be safeguarded.

Make-believe

Learning to make-believe is achieved through opportunity to practise with children and others who already know the ropes. Contrary to what had been supposed in the past, research now indicates that make-believe is not simply a matter of doing what comes naturally. Children are *introduced* to the basics by members of their families (Garvey, 1991). When coaxing a reluctant toddler to eat, a parent or other family member will offer a spoonful to the teddy bear, with much lip-smacking and yum-yumming. Sometimes after a fall, the teddy bear gets a bandaged leg to match that of the injured child. The child is given a comforting sweet and one for 'poor old teddy bear'. The fact that teddy cannot eat leads to a suggestion: 'Pretend he can.' Older brothers and sisters often tutor their younger siblings in make-believe play, telling them what to say and do. Early years practitioners contribute to the induction process by huffing and puffing at imaginary candles on clay birthday cakes and tucking in to sand

Making connections: older and younger children, together

dished up in buckets as breakfast, with spades for spoons. Practitioners sometimes use puppets to introduce the idea of getting into role and becoming the puppet character. Sometimes they sit with a child who is not yet joining in and interpret what is going on: 'Look at Tariq and Clare pretending to be naughty babies and here comes Mave, pretending she's cross with them.' The word 'pretend' is a key word in the language of play and essential to successful social interaction amongst children.

Stories

During the period of preparation for the new rule, Paley created a story which unfolded from day to day, to support the thinking of her own group of five- and six-year-olds. Like many parents and early childhood educators, Vivian Paley is an ardent believer in the power of stories to engage children's thoughts and feelings. She sees a relationship between the folktales, myths and fairytales handed down from generation to generation and the fantasies which children make up for themselves in their make-believe play. The thread linking the two are the universal and pervasive human concerns of: identity, relationships, friendship, belonging, rejection, contribution, justice, strength and weakness, power, control and lack of it, safety and danger, triumph and disaster, lost and found.

In her writing, Paley reminds us of the power of stories to create pathways connecting people to each other. In children's play we see this process of connecting occurring as children take from each other's lives, from the stories we tell them, the special events and outings we arrange, from television and storybooks, and then as they weave new, shared stories.

Parents

Where parents and families are seen as genuinely part of the group, they can contribute very powerfully to the creation of an *extended* amiable circle of change and development. Parents are frequent visitors to Vivian Paley's classroom and are particularly welcome as storytellers. She encourages them to tell stories of their childhood and the children are invited to perform them (Paley, 1995). Many adults in our increasingly multicultural society were born and spent their childhood in countries far from where they now live. Tales of these childhoods are a rich and diverse strand of experience for children to enjoy, reflect on and relate to.

Adults as well as children can discover their common humanity with others through the sharing of stories about childhood. As a tutor in adult education, I have found that sharing such stories has proved to be a very powerful way of helping create an amiable circle of adult learners. On one occasion, a playgroup course member, born in The Gambia, West Africa told us about her childhood. Her grand*mother* was the village chieftain, who knew everything about everything and was very strict – with everyone. The centrepiece of Mary's story was her description of the passing on from one generation to another of the customs involved in gathering water from the river:

> *Each day, it was the job of the older boys and girls of the village to look after their younger brothers and sisters and also to fetch water from the river. The river was tidal and at low tide mud-flats were exposed either side of the water. The older children taught the younger how to make a waterhole by scooping out a hollow in the mud and decorating the rim with pebbles, sticks, grasses and flower-heads. Sometimes they brought with them special bits and pieces to add to the decorative finish of the waterholes. There was great rivalry to produce the most beautiful arrangement. 'My grandmother played that same game, and my mother, when they were children.' Mary told us. On returning to the river the next day, again at low tide, the waterholes would be full of water and the decorations gone. The older children told the younger ones the river had taken the flowers and left the water as payment.*

As soon as Mary had finished her story there was a chorus of recognition. The points of contact with others were many: grannies who were chieftains in all but name; minding younger children and other child-labours and several stories about the making of decorative, miniature gardens. Picking up on Mary's story, Fay who was brought up in an inner-city suburb of south London, told us how she and others used to make peep-show grottoes inside shoe boxes, using earth, flower-heads, sticks, shells and scraps of silver cigarette paper for the obligatory pool and miniature plaster statues of the Virgin Mary. With a lid over the top to hide the contents, the children would position themselves by the entrance to the local greyhound racing stadium to catch the punters, who played their part in this local tradition by paying for a peep according to their opinion of the artistry involved. 'This was our way of making a bit of pocket money,' she explained.

Fay's story, like Mary's before her, rang bells for many others . . . and so it went, with each story building on the one before. The process was very like the way in which young children's group play develops from one moment to the next and from day to day.

Group discussion

Opportunity for small groups to come together to make plans, share stories and reflect on their lives and learning is generally agreed to be an important part of the daily programme. Many practitioners think it is better for the same group of children to meet together with the same adult, than to keep chopping and changing. The size of group needs to be just right, neither so big as to make genuine discussion unlikely, nor too small to throw up challenges. Children are often divided according to age for their small-group meeting and there is a lot to be said for this. Equally, advantages can be seen in mixed-age groups where the younger children can learn from their older companions and where the older ones have to think about making themselves intelligible to the younger members of the group.

In addition to the content of the meeting, this is an opportunity for children to learn the rules of discussion:

- only one person to speak at a time

- everyone else to listen

Also needed are:

- a means of signalling a wish to speak

- a means of signalling who has the floor

They need to learn that discussion is not about everyone getting a turn to speak about any old thing but of listening and responding to what is being said. It is the adult's job to ensure the fair distribution of turns and that the children are 'hearing' each other by occasionally asking 'Do you mean . . . ?' At the end of the discussion the adult should sum up with reference to what the children have said and adding a personal comment as appropriate. The aim, as with all these support strategies, is to help children connect with each other in order to further their understandings of each other as members of the amiable circle.

SUMMARY

In this chapter the idea of the group as an amiable circle of change and development has been considered and contrasted with its opposite: a vicious circle. The latter was seen as the consequence of the rejecting behaviours of some members of the group towards others. The opportunities for children to reflect on their relationships through the introduction of a rule and the back-up to support children in dealing with the consequences, provided the main focus of this chapter.

The following questions may help you tune in to the social climate of your group.

- Do time and space arrangements encourage freedom of movement and interaction?

- Are some children persistently excluded from the freely chosen activities of others?

- Are there persistent excluders?

- Can you explain either of these?

- Are there children who do not join in? Can you explain this? Does it matter?

- Are there children who have not even one friend? If so, how are they affected?

- Would you adopt a blanket approach to problems connected with the social climate of the group, or treat cases individually?

- Do you genuinely discuss things together?

8 BOUGHT AND FOUND

INTRODUCTION

A girl and boy of about nine or ten years old are minding a two-year-old. They are at the water's edge on a rocky outcrop jutting into the sea. The older children are skimming stones and the two-year-old is choosing large rocks to drop into the water. The older children keep half an eye, as they too hunt for the right kind of stones for their game. It is a wonder the younger child doesn't hurl himself into the water, given that he has to aim each heavy rock away from himself and release it at exactly the right moment. The game goes on for about fifteen minutes. It is difficult to decide whether the two-year-old is interested in the clatter of rock against rock as each one makes its descent before splashing into the water a few feet away; or whether he is intent on filling the sea, or is it the sheer physicality of the activity that grips him so totally? A voice calls to the older children to fetch the younger. They try, but are ignored. He simply goes on with his game. 'He won't come,' they shout back to the voice. 'Tell him we're going to buy toys,' says the voice, 'that'll fetch him.'

In this chapter, the relative merits of bought and found materials are explored and their differences reconciled.

TOYS

In a pilot project for an ongoing Europe-wide study of children and toys based at the Nordic Centre for Research on Toys and Educational Media, an audit of toys owned by eight-year-olds revealed an average of 700 items. Items which formed part of a collection were counted individually, so, for example, three farm animal replicas would count as three items but a Lego brick would be counted as part of a larger whole not as a single item (Krister Svensson, CFL University of Halmsted, Sweden, personal communication). The analysis is not yet complete, but the figure itself may not come as a surprise to many parents in Europe.

Toys, as my opening observation suggests, have a significance in the lives of children and their families which go beyond the particulars of any single item.

The same toy takes on a different significance in the context of the playgroup or school. Children play with some toys in school which parents tell us they never touch at home. They may also play with them differently. This is why toys cannot be recommended for school use simply because they have been used successfully at home and vice versa. Nor, by the same token could they be actively not recommended.

Toys as property

Parents with whom I have discussed toys admit that from time to time toys are used between themselves and their children as currency to buy co-operation in advance or reward it retrospectively. At home a child's toys are regarded and respected as personal property by both child and family. Parental incursions into the toybox with a view to weeding out redundant items are viewed as a violation of sovereign rights by parents as well as children. Trading old for new is a different matter. Parents who override their children's property rights, because they think a clear-out is overdue, do so in the dead of night, without permission. They hope that the children will not miss whatever it is. They do. When a friend comes to play, a parent has to arbitrate between the rights of guests and the rights of owners. Own toys act as social currency between children: if it's your toy, you make the rules; failure to co-operate leads to threat of, or actual withdrawal of the toy. When the guest is the owner, parental diplomacy is stretched to the limit.

Personal toys

In considering the significance of children's own toys we need to distinguish between toy ownership and *personal* toys. Some toys acquire deep personal meanings for children which are sometimes beyond our understanding but which we must recognise and respect and go out of our way to keep track of and protect.

'Found' versus 'bought'

As an early childhood educator, I was a little sad as the two-year-old on the beach was lured away from his absorbing game with the bribe of toys. Later, in a more reflective mood, I conceded it wasn't the bribe, as such, that bothered me. That, as a parent, I could understand. It was the natural status of the child's 'found' material versus the 'bought' and 'manufactured' status of what was being offered. I have an antipathy to toys which is not entirely rational. It has something to do with my background in early childhood education which tends to idealise natural materials for reasons I will try to explain later.

There is no *inherent* reason why a toy should be any less absorbing to a child than something found. As this theme developed in my mind, I thought about the hundreds of items which comprised our own children's toy collections and began remembering why it was so difficult for them to sort out their stuff into two piles: Stuff I Use / Stuff I Don't. This exercise was usually carried out on the basis that Stuff I Don't would be donated to children who had no toys (moral blackmail). Stuff I Don't is a figment of the adult imagination. The reason everything ends up in the Stuff I Use pile is because children mix and match their toys just as they mix sand and water together to make something new. This explains why their toyboxes or rooms are always such a mess. From seven hundred items they may create seven times seven hundred different games.

If ownership means that children are free to use their toys in their own way, within limits of safety, there seems no reason why they cannot be as valuable a source of learning as found and natural materials. Resourceful children find ways to combine the two, with toys and natural materials extending each other.

Timeless and durable

Materials like sand, water, earth, clay and stones are timeless and durable. Their found status makes them the common property of the human race. It is this which enables us to see links in children's play with our human past and across cultures. An example of this is prehistoric and early dry-stone building where the basic configurations used by our ancestors are exactly the same as those used by children in blockplay: lines, planes, enclosures and envelopments. I experienced an example whilst walking in the limestone wilderness of The Burren in the west of Ireland when we came across a prehistoric megalith made from two standing stones with a third stone bridging the two. Surrounding this as far as the eye could see were miniature replica megaliths, made by visitors, perhaps in homage to the past, from the loose material of the surrounding landscape. Many different techniques had been used to make the stones stand upright and connected in these mini-megaliths. It was like being back in the nursery block area.

Durable materials, timeless forms

THE CHILD IN THE GARDEN

Froebel (1782–1852) felt that a garden in which young children could immerse themselves in the natural world was the ideal learning environment. A garden represents a system of interrelationships between living and non-living forms and processes. The garden symbolises agriculture which, like others, he saw as the beginning of modern civilisation. By tilling the earth, growing plants and caring for animals children could become more fully human. Digging was seen as rather special, partly, one suspects, because it symbolises honest toil.

From a Froebelian perspective, natural materials as found in field and garden are seen as the bottom line in terms of human adaptation to the environment. Knowledge of them is therefore seen as the foundation of all future learning.

Due to the passage of time, Froebel's garden has been pulled up by the roots, as it were, the parts separated from the whole. What we have in its place today are 'natural materials' presented out of context, as separate items. The connection of the parts to the whole are gone, – unless we are prepared to let children reconnect them in ways which make sense to *them* rather than to *our* sense of order, as they do with their toys at home.

Materials provide the means for giving external expression and form to ideas

MATERIALS AS TOOLS OF THOUGHT

The effect of separating the parts from the whole has resulted in an emphasis on the *matter* of materials, that is, on water as water, sand as sand. Whilst this is important, it has served to obscure the fact that children use stuff, including toys, as *tools* to think with about the world of ideas, feelings, imaginings, events, people and places beyond the here and now. As tools of thought, materials provide the means for giving external expression and form to their ideas. Once ideas are given material form, they can be looked at, worked on and refined. This is the basis of Malaguzzi's suggestion, discussed in Chapter 1: that different materials are like different 'languages'; without them children are rendered 'speechless'. Children need to know about the matter of materials so that they can become experts in using them to think with.

Naming activities

Research indicates that children make much more complex use of materials than can be imagined by the labels we attach to activities: blockplay, sandplay, painting. It seems that by using these forms of words, we may be missing the fact that the material is only one dimension of the activity. Knowledge, non-verbal and verbal transaction, make-believe, wordplay, movement, problem-solving, exploration and materials may all be woven together to form a single, coherent episode of play. It would make just as much sense to call it by any of these other elements as to call it by the name of the material being used. Close observation reveals this richness and complexity (Reifel and Yeatman, 1993). Consider the ingredients which make up this episode:

> *Mark is using blocks. James, Elaine and Tim are nearby:*
>
> *Mark:* I'm going to make Big Ben . . . *(rapidly builds a tower which collapses)* Big Ben fell down . . . that's like London Bridge . . . I'm going to build it again . . . *(aside to Elaine) Elaine, my fish is dead . . . (all four children talk about fish and dying).*
>
> *Tim tells the others that his little sister, who goes to playgroup, had been* dying *to go to the toilet and had wet her knickers before she got there:*
>
> *Tim:* She was dying to go . . . not dying like when you're dead . . . *(clutches himself by the throat and makes last gasp noises to demonstrate the difference).*
>
> *Mark, meanwhile, has resumed building Big Ben:*
>
> *Mark:* Ding-dong, ding-dong.
>
> *Elaine:* I don't like Big Ben.
>
> *Mark:* I do. Don't say that. Why did you say it's silly? Ding-dong, ding-dong . . . I went into the clock shop yesterday and bought a grandmother clock and it went Ting! Ting!
>
> *James: (hovering teasingly over Mark's series of towers)* I can bust it down.
>
> *Mark:* It's not funny . . . *(builds another, taller tower)* This is the Prime Minister . . . No . . . She lives in there . . . *(points to one of his towers)* in Big Ben.

SCHEMAS

If we are interested in making connections with our human past, schemas may be the vital link. These are the basic mental frameworks discussed in Chapter 3, which make up the system which kickstarts the process of interaction between the individual mind and the environment (Piaget, 1951). It may be that these basic frameworks have remained the same since the dawn of humankind and this is why we can detect similarities between things like megalithic structures and children's blockplay. Points, lines, boundaries, connection, enclosure, envelopment are all examples of schema. All occur in blockplay and all occur in the early dry-stone building of our ancestors. What is even more interesting is that these same concerns can be seen to cut *across* materials, lending weight to the idea of universality. If we are looking for connections between our human past and the world we live in today, schemas may be a promising way to go. Schemas make no distinction between natural and manufactured materials, everything is grist to the mill of learning.

Practical implications

Allowing children to make connections as if in a garden means some rethinking of the boundaries between activities to make them more permeable. This needs to be worked out with colleagues and children. There is more of this in Chapter 11. A promising development in playgroups, nurseries and schools are workshop areas stocked with all manner of stuff, lots of it expendable, for using freely, separately and in combination. With this kind of provision children can mix materials and textures, shapes and forms as they connect ideas together to create new wholes.

SUMMARY

The significance of toys depends to some extent on whether ownership is with an individual child in the family or with a group, as in school. Although there are many moral issues tied up with individual ownership, it was not the purpose of the chapter to expose these. A *virtue* of ownership may be children's freedom to adapt toys to suit their own purposes.

The holistic idea of the garden as the ideal setting for learning has been fragmented in recent times. Unless ways can be found of enabling children to make connections between parts to create new wholes, the significance of natural materials as powerful learning tools is reduced.

Close observation of children using materials suggests greater complexity than is conveyed when we refer to an activity by the name of the material being used.

Finally, schemas were suggested as a connecting link between our human past and the present.

9 SHELLING PEAS: WORK OR PLAY OR WHAT?

INTRODUCTION

Play is universally acknowledged to be of great significance to children across cultures whilst work is seen as the preoccupation of adults. Adults have the job of steering children towards adulthood and many see this as a cue for hitting the fast-forward button, putting work before play in the education of young children.

In this chapter the educational consequences of the visible and hidden messages which children receive about work and play are considered, with reference to research into children's own views.

CHILDREN'S VIEWS

Increasingly, researchers are getting alongside children to try to discover how they interpret their nursery and school experiences. The methods they use are interesting. First they talk generally with the children about what they do in school, what they like and dislike. The idea is to avoid putting words like 'work' and 'play' into their mouths and allow them to frame their own descriptions. The researcher listens carefully to the *way* in which children refer to their institutional experiences. From this, key terms are identified and these become the focus of further study and discussion. In two studies using this method (Robson, 1993; Wing, 1995) children between the ages of three and eight years overwhelmingly characterised their experiences in their institutional settings in terms of *work* and *play*.

Once these terms had been introduced *by the children*, Wing combined observation with further in-depth interviews with six- and seven-year-old children in two classes. First, she observed the children in the classroom, then, referring to what she had seen, would ask whether that was work or play and what made it so. The findings from both the Robson and Wing studies are very similar and have been combined in the following summary.

Work or play?

For children, work is:

- compulsory

- teacher-initiated, owned and directed

- concerned with teacher intentions only – tasks are done for the teacher not the self

- 'hard' and involves mental effort; mathematics, reading and writing are usually implicated

- related to learning

- teacher-intensive; involves helping, monitoring and evaluating

- tasks which have a finishing point determined by the teacher, usually involving a product or result

- usually solitary

- often enjoyable, sometimes fun

- never sacrificed to play

It is important to remember that in Wing's study (the more intensive of the two), the children's descriptions were based on actual classroom experiences observed by the researcher. The settings studied by both Robson and Wing were staffed by adults who believed play was vital to young children's learning. Many of the activities which had what the children saw as worklike characteristics were intended as invitations to play by the adults. 'Structured play' involving tasks determined by the adult would thus be experienced by the children as work.

Play

In contrast to work, play was for the self. It involved:

- options

- children not teachers (this should be read as an observation by the children rather than an imperative)

- children's priorities and intentions

- 'ownership' by children

- self-determination

- choice of content and companions

- freedom to decide the finishing point and to drop in and out

- physical movement

- less mental effort than work

- doing things that were not about learning

- equality in the distribution of power

- enjoyment and on occasions fun

They saw play as subordinate to work in terms of teacher priorities, as something which must give way to work but never the reverse.

Wing was surprised at the characterisation of play as involving less mental effort than work. She writes (ibid. p.235):

Children's planning, decision-making and problem-solving activities were evident in observations of play activities. Elaborate schemes in sand and blockplay and intense concentration in self-selected drawing activities were apparent. However, children seemed unaware of any cognitive demand.

This comment speaks volumes about the difference between work and play from children's perspectives. In *both* work and play they were seen to engage in cognitively demanding tasks which in the compulsory situation they described as hard, but not in the self-determining one. They also seem to equate learning only with the things which teachers are interested in. Since teachers were seen as paying little attention to their play, they concluded play is not about learning. It takes very little imagination to see how the idea of play as a pleasant but worthless, unproductive pursuit persists as part of the public consciousness.

Another of Wing's findings was that depending on whether the teacher or child was seen to be in charge, the *same* activity could change from work to play or play to work. Children often *chose* to read, write and engage in mathematical activities for pleasure and therefore classed this as play-like.

There was little suggestion that they categorically disliked work. Enjoyment was often mentioned in relation to it.

In-between activities

Both Robson and Wing noted that despite these broad characterisations of work and play, there were many activities which children were reluctant to label one way or the other. They obviously found the two words inadequate to encompass the range of possibilities between what they described as 'pure' work and 'pure' play. It seems that the older children in Wing's study became more reflective about work and play as a result of the discussions they had with her, which made it increasingly difficult to assign activities in sharply contrasting terms.

Wing suggests that early childhood educators might take on board the more developed and differentiated view of activities which began to emerge from her study. The more complex web of relationships perceived by the children between work and play may be a more effective model in terms of curriculum planning than the more traditional and simplistic work–play distinction. Creating situations which combine elements of both work and play is very different from 'structured play' which is an *adult* construct. Wing proposes a fusing of adult and child perspectives so as to create increased opportunities for the meeting of minds and sense of shared purpose, or reciprocity. This would involve adults in taking children's play as seriously as children are expected to take work, and becoming involved in it on children's terms. In the next section we look at a range of possibilities for reciprocal activity.

RECIPROCAL ACTIVITY

Playing with children

Playing with children is not about intervening in play to make teaching points. This, as we have seen, would change the situation from play to work. In play, action and direction is determined by agreement between the players, and anyone who does not like the way things are going can try to redirect the course of action through negotiation – or drop out. This differs from the teaching situation where one person holds all the cards. The teacher knows more about the subject or skill which has to be learned and the steps to be taken. The process is not open to negotiation or opting out. In play, the adult does not necessarily know more than the children. Margaret Gracie (1977) describes how she joined a group engaged in their current craze for making Lego animals. As she had never played with Lego before, she sought advice from one of the children on the basic principles of construction. The child was reluctant at first, seeming to doubt her sincerity. She was genuinely pleased with her completed elephant and enjoyed the children's praise. In addition to learning about Lego, she learned from the experience (p.85):

Even five-year-olds know things that they can teach to adults (and other children).

Responding to play on children's terms

After further experience as a co-player with other groups of children, Gracie summarises the learning involved in conventional academic terms, but suggests of equal importance is the effect on teacher–pupil relationships resulting from adult involvement as co-player. The children learn that adults can share and contribute to play by participating as one of the group, with a common purpose. Her conclusion is that if playing together is a genuinely shared experience, there is no need for the adult to spell out the learning to the children.

Work or play or both

In one of the schools involved in Robson's study, children referred less frequently to activities in terms of work and play. They seemed to see their nursery experiences as largely self-determined. In fact, the children in this setting were not free to do as they pleased, when they pleased. It may be that there was an underlying spirit of shared purpose which blurred the distinctions children perceived in the other settings. Or it may be that the adults employed characteristics usually associated with play during 'teaching' encounters with children. These would include:

- transaction or exchange, rather than a one-way flow

- reciprocity, which is to do with sharing control of an exchange, tuning in and staying tuned to each other's verbal and non-verbal signals

- accepting many possible ways of seeing things, and understanding that what makes sense is not always subject to rational analysis

- acknowledging the many symbolic 'languages' of early childhood, rather than the few

- valuing process as well as product, so that children are not focused on getting a result at the expense of learning

- sharing ownership of ideas, intentions and purposes

- taking cues from the children about what is worth pursuing

- replying to children's contributions rather than evaluating them

- being prepared to employ imaginary scenarios, such as make-believe and stories, to make difficult ideas more accessible

Can I do that?

There is an intriguing area of activity which is difficult to classify from either a work or play perspective. Activities in this area often occur in the home setting, are high on goal structure and often involve a product. They are freely chosen and experienced by children with great intensity and involvement. These are the activities engaged in by adults, which grab and hold children's attention and in which they beg to be involved: 'Can I do that?'. Shelling peas springs to mind. A vivid early childhood recollection of mine is of kneeling at the kitchen table opposite my mother, a pile of peas for shelling between us.

Work or play?

There was so much to think about: the scent and sound of pea pods popping, each containing a surprise; how many were in a pod, how fat, how green, how maggoty; some looking full to bursting, others flat and unpoppable; how to shoot the peas from their shells in one deft movement. There was lots of conferring across the table about which peas were titchy enough to be eaten on the spot – a pea-podder's privilege. Other activities in this category include stripping wallpaper, painting walls, working with wood, making jam buns and apple pies, digging the garden, washing up, scrubbing tables, polishing furniture, playing cards and dominoes, sewing and knitting, picking blackberries. Perhaps you can think of some from your own childhood?

Why are such activities so attractive to children? Is it something to do with seeing an operation or activity performed with skill? There is an aesthetic about any skilled performance in any area of human activity which is irresistible. It is my hunch that a trained eye is not needed to spot such a performance. Maybe a skilled performance looks so good that it taps into the young child's urge to be 'able', and thus acts as a strong motivating force.

Many of the activities mentioned are high on sensory appeal: children seeing someone turn over a spadeful of earth are drawn as much by the appearance and imagined feel of the earth as the performance of the digger. All the activities have the power to engage children's minds.

Children may wish to penetrate the bubble of concentration which envelops the performer, to be part of that person's world rather than excluded from it. Participation in such activity involves common purposes which lead to common understandings, as well as the opportunity to make a helping contribution. Are there lessons we can take from this kind of activity to apply in our schools?

SUMMARY

Children's characterisations of work and play hinge on questions of choice, control, ownership and involvement. When these are in the hands of children, tasks are seen to involve less mental effort and learning than work. Maybe we need to encourage choice, control and ownership by relinquishing some of ours and becoming more involved in their play, on their terms. This could lead to some redefinition of work and play on both sides. Wings' study takes account of variations in emphasis between worklike and playlike activities and offers a possible way forward.

10 Enquiry-based Practice I: Fish Out Of Water

Introduction

Enquiry-based practice is a way of working which takes nothing for granted. It is concerned with the continuous process of reducing the gap between principles and practice, the familiar and unfamiliar, the expected and unexpected. The integrity of the developmental approach depends on the recognition that enquiry into our own practice is not an option but a necessary way of working with young children. It is the way in which we contribute to the amiable circle of change and development.

In Chapter 5, I referred to early childhood educators as fish in water. Enquiry-based practice requires us to get out of the water so that we can see it. In this and the final chapter, we look at strategies for reviewing our principles and practice from the outside looking in.

Problem-solving

Sometimes we are pushed into thinking about aspects of practice because a problem has arisen. It may be a health and care issue, raised by parents, such as worries about wet shoes and water play. Runny noses and the price of a good pair of shoes must be as much the concern of practitioners as of parents. We need to observe water play to find out why children's shoes get soaked. Is it anything to do with the height of the water tray not being perfect for everyone; or water running off waterproof aprons? Is it to do with the containers used in the water tray?

Often we make use of recycled containers, without checking what happens when children use them. Sometimes a bottle is so large that it cannot be gripped, lifted, and aimed in a controlled way, when full of water. This is equivalent to giving a young child a pair of dressmaking scissors to cut out magazine pictures; or a bike to someone whose feet barely reach the pedals. Is there anything in the tray, like a housebrick, which could be used as a surface on which to rest a container as it is being filled? Or do they have to manipulate two containers in mid-air, the one to be filled and the other to pour from? Do the children know they are spilling water outside the water tray?

Playing devil's advocate

Sometimes a provocative statement can stop us in our tracks and make us question our assumptions. This was the effect when, for the sake of argument, I suggested to a group of students that in the interests of equal opportunities, all dolls should be removed from educational settings (1). The idea emerged as we were discussing the need for care in ensuring that all peoples are reflected in our provision for learning. We looked particularly closely at anti-racist literature (2) and wondered whether there could ever be a wide enough range of skin tones and facial characteristics for someone, somewhere, not to recognise themselves. The students were asked to look at the children they work with, at the dolls provided and the use made of them. The responses were surprising and even more thought-provoking than my original proposition:

> What about the children in leg braces and wheelchairs; those who walk with the help of a walking frame, who wear a hearing aid and glasses, or head gear; those with visible birthmarks; those of restricted growth; of above average girth; with the characteristic features of a Down's syndrome child? (3)

Children's free incorporation of dolls into their play was less frequent than expected, even where these had been sensitively chosen to reflect diversity. Children used each other as their children more frequently than they used dolls. They were seen tucking up a variety of objects including a pair of trains (observed at home) and a plastic duck (nursery). Cots were found stripped of bedding and filled with pots and pans. Pushchairs and prams were used as general purpose vehicles. Doll nakedness was endemic. In one group, where the dolls were removed for a week, no-one mentioned the fact. No boys were observed playing with dolls even though realistic male dolls were provided. Although this was seen as a cause for concern by members of the group, it has to be considered in the light of the fact that the ethnically differentiated dolls were not used much either. Where dolls *were* used by the children, this tended to be centred around themed activities set up by adults, like hospital and clinic play and bathing routines.

This was not an in-depth study and left us with more questions than answers, which members of the group would continue to pursue in their own way and according to their circumstances and purposes. The observations which emerged do not offer grounds for *not* providing dolls as diverse as we can buy or make them. However, it is possible that realism is only one factor in children's relationships with dolls. It may be that dolls serve different purposes depending on whether the setting is home or school. It would be interesting to collaborate with parents in a comparative study of doll play at home and school and to include observations of children younger than three, since we only looked at children from three to six years. When did you last look at doll-use in your setting?

A SURVEY OF RESOURCES

To discover whether our aims for children are being met, we can conduct a systematic survey of resources for learning, bearing in mind that these include space and time as well as people and stuff. The aim of such a survey is to discover what is being used, when and by whom. This can be done by the relatively simple process of timed mapping.

Materials

- you need several dozen A4 size copies of the layout of your room or rooms and the outdoor space if this applies. Ideally each room and outdoor space should be on separate sheets so that you don't have to cramp your notes.

Method

- Use one sheet per room for every time check.

- Enter the time and date on each sheet.

- Indicate on each sheet whether the children were free to be in or out of doors or either at the time of the observation.

- At *regular, timed intervals* (for example, once every 15–20 minutes) start at one end of the room and work towards the other end. Without rushing, mark on your plan who is in each activity area, using children's initials. Don't worry if someone leaves the room before you get to them, just leave

DATE	TIME	IN/OUT	OBSERVER

Books   Workshops

Home Area

Puzzles

Construction

Blocks

Water

Easels   Sink

Sand

Room Map

Work from one end to another. Use initials to identify which children are at which location at time of scan.

him or her out. If a parent or colleague is helping you with this, who does not know all the children's names, ask them simply to note the total number of boys and girls separately for each activity.

- Do the same in any other rooms and outdoor space to which children have free access, or ask colleagues in those other areas to do this.

- Do this for one week. To make comparisons easier from day to day, try to keep as near as possible to the same times and intervals each day. If you miss a 'turn', forget it and wait for the next turn to come round.

The mapping of activities takes only a few minutes, on each turn, per room or space.

Review

Review your records daily otherwise it becomes an onerous task:

1   Are there activities that are more or less popular? If possible put them in order of popularity.

2   How do the figures break down in terms of age and gender?

3   Is time of day a factor in what seems to be popular or not?

4   Are there any noticeable patterns in relation to individual children?

5   What is the effect of *having to be indoors* compared to *having a choice of indoors or out* on children's choice of activity?

6   Any other points?

At the end of the week put your daily reviews together to see the whole picture and make a note of anything which grabs your attention.

Repeat

In two weeks' time, without changing anything in the meantime, repeat the survey for a further week, reflecting on your observations as you go and making notes. You may find the picture changing in some respects during this second period of observation, due to the passage of time. Some aspects may appear unchanged. By the time your observations are completed for the two periods, questions will have begun to form, some of which you will want to follow up.

Consult colleagues

If the survey is carried out as a joint staff venture, decisions about what to do with your findings will be taken together. There is a better chance of bringing about change and development if this can be done collaboratively. In any case, it is important to communicate your findings to colleagues, so that they are aware of any concerns you have and of any plans for further enquiry and/or action.

ACTION–ENQUIRY

As a result of your survey, you may decide to look more closely at a particular area of provision which you think needs some input. The following approach, using a combination of questioning, action and reflection may be useful to you. The sequence referred to here was worked out during a review of blockplay carried out in a nursery involving the age range 0–5.

1   Set aside some time each day, for a week or so, to *observe* and *describe* the provision, without taking part.

2   After observing and describing, the next step is to identify *possible goals for action*. Taking blockplay as an example, these might include any of the following:

- raising the status of blockplay
- ensuring equality of access
- encouraging co-operation and collaboration
- raising awareness of the mathematical and aesthetic characteristics of the blocks and the forms which can be made with them
- encouraging investigation and problem-solving
- encouraging constructional uses of blocks
- encouraging children to look at the built environment and raise awareness of pattern in the environment
- encouraging development in the structural complexity of constructions to include two- and three-dimensional forms
- developing methods of recording children's blockplay
- developing blockplay with the 0–3-year-olds

3   Choose just *one* of these as a starting point.

4   Draw up a *plan of action* including any strategies you might try. In the case of blocks this might include: planning for an adult to spend time in the block area; restricting the use of blocks to the block area; re-organising the presentation of blocks.

5   Try just *one* of these strategies to begin with, otherwise you will lose track of possible causes for any subsequent change and development. *Observe and record* the effects over several days. Don't be in too much of a hurry to write off a strategy as sometimes it takes a week or so for any changes to take effect.

6   Stand back to *consider the effects* and go back, either to step **2** or **4**, bearing in mind what you now know.

IN-DEPTH CHILD STUDY

Child study has a long and celebrated history in early childhood education. You may want to use this as a way of looking closely at one child and at your provision and approach simultaneously.

Who?

If your mapping survey did not throw up questions about an individual child, make a random choice of child by sticking a pin in the register, or put the children's names into a hat and draw one out.

Finding a starting point

Observe the child with an open mind for two or three days, noting interests, social patterns such as relationships with children and any special friendships, relationships with adults and responses to adult-led and compulsory activities; collect samples of painting, drawing, early writing; note any activity with three-dimensional materials and patterns of physical activity.

From this, decide on a more specific focus. Whatever you choose as a starting point, it is guaranteed to lead to other aspects of the whole child and a re-evaluation of principles and practice.

Observe and record

Try to make daily observations and record these on the spot, or as soon as possible, in note form. You may want to devise your own recording sheets, or simply use blank pages and a loose-leaf binder.

- Remember to include the date and time of recording.

- If you find yourself pressed for time, use time sampling. This involves a few minutes observation at regularly spaced intervals. If nothing else, you can check what the child is doing and with whom.

- Longer periods of observation are best done with the co-operation of colleagues.

Reflection

Reflect on your observations to see where they might be leading.

- Look for connections with other aspects of the whole child, with this child and other children.

- Be prepared to take your queries to the child who will be pleased you asked and try to help.

- Colleagues can also be used as sounding boards for your reflections.

Interpretation

The more detail you can get into your study the better chance you have of being able to understand what you are describing. The anthropologist Clifford Geertz

(1973) writes of the need for events and behaviour to be described with all the surrounding details painted in. He refers to this as 'thick description'. We need enough information, he suggests, to be able to distinguish a cheeky wink from a nervous blink.

Play

Play is seen by many as a context in which children reveal themselves. This is not to say we can watch children at play and immediately understand what it means to them. We need frameworks which can help us make intelligent guesses about what particular play episodes mean to the children involved. The best frameworks are those produced by painstaking research. In the past, much of this has come from the fields of developmental psychology, paediatrics and sociology. Useful as these can be, they have not tended to reflect meanings from the children's point of view. Sometimes research has been done in situations especially set up for the purpose and does not reflect the everyday circumstances children are used to at home and in school. These days, children are increasingly being studied in the context of their lives, with parents and practitioners participating.

In using 'thick description' to document a child at play in your home, playgroup, nursery or early years classroom, you will contribute to the extension and development of your own frameworks for understanding children's play and possibly of other people, if you share your material more widely.

Vivian Paley, whose work has been discussed in other chapters, is a practitioner researcher who makes extensive use of a tape-recorder to capture children's conversations and play dialogues. After school she listens to what has been recorded and makes a note of anything she doesn't understand. The following day, she asks the children concerned for clarification. Sometimes she takes an issue arising from the tapes and makes this the subject of a small group discussion aimed at helping her get on the inside of children's thinking and concerns. When we study individual children *in context*, we also study the context.

Summary

In this chapter the meaning and implications of enquiry-based practice have been discussed. In describing strategies for reviewing principles and practice it is difficult to avoid over-simplification. Putting them into practice is far less ordered than might appear on paper. Trying to keep to a system and moving one step at a time is advice worth hanging on to. Even if you can manage this, from time to time you will lose your bearings and feel down-hearted and wonder whether it is worthwhile. At other times you will take strength from the fact that you know you can make a difference.

Making time for observation and action–enquiry is dealt with in the final chapter.

Notes

(1) This summary is based on material lent me by Judy Evans, Helen Fensterheim, Gilli Pettinger, Ian Taylor and Sue Wadhams.

(2) This material is produced by the Working Group Against Racism in Children's Resources, 460, Wandsworth Road, London, SW8 3LX.

(3) Dolls with disability aids such as wheelchairs, crutches and walking frames are listed in the Nottingham Rehab catalogue, Ludlow Hill Road, West Bridgford, Nottingham NG2 6HD. Tel: 0115 945 2345.

11 ENQUIRY-BASED PRACTICE II: SPACE AND TIME

INTRODUCTION

Our organisation of time and space should support the pursuit of our aims for children in ways consistent with our beliefs. From a developmental perspective these emphasise informality, interaction, degrees of freedom and control, interest and curiosity, purpose, involvement. They suggest that learning is a process of connecting and constructing and involves give and take. Relationships between people are of central importance, contributing as they do to an individual's sense of belonging and providing the most powerful of all learning resources. All of these principles are implicated in the way we use time and space:

> those crucial classroom features that have become so routine as to have slipped from awareness.
>
> (McAuley, 1990 p.91)

The purpose of this final chapter is to raise awareness of issues of time and space.

WASTED TIME

An inescapable fact of enquiry-based practice is that it requires practitioners to be free to observe and interact with children. Research suggests, however, that we spend disproportionate amounts of time on petty management compared to that spent playing and working with the children (Bruner, 1980). Rather than hotly denying this we can check for ourselves. How much time do you spend:

• helping children with clothing of one sort or another, including protective clothing • changing children's clothing because the protective clothing doesn't protect • mopping up spills • sweeping up sand • monitoring turn-taking • removing wet paintings from easels, hanging them to dry and putting up fresh paper • handing out materials • helping children find materials • tidying up after children • giving children instructions • supervising transitions from one part of the timetable or room to another • settling children for story or circle time • lecturing children about noise, rushing about and interfering with others • preparing materials like dough and paints • washing up paint pots and brushes • scrubbing tables?

When we are caught up in this kind of activity, not only do we reduce the amount of time for enquiry, playing and working with children, we loose track of our aims. These include helping children take increasing control of their lives, the development of self-discipline and regard for others.

Reclaiming time for all

Many of the tasks we assign ourselves are wasteful of children's time as well as ours. To reduce our own list of time wasters we need to conduct a series of mini enquiries beginning with: 'Why am I doing this?' followed by: 'Could this be organised so that the children could help themselves more?'

Child sufficiency

Children learn at different rates. The younger they are the more they need to follow their own unique pathways to the same goals, starting with what they already know. One way to accommodate the differences between children is to organise the environment so that with our guidance, they can match their present knowledge and understanding to appropriately challenging learning situations.

This means organising the physical environment for child-sufficiency rather than dependency on adults. Maude Brown (1990, 1991a, 1991b) advises that the best way to create a child-sufficient environment is to consult the children about the layout of the room, the care and display of materials, storage and labelling. Tidying up routines also need to be talked through. When children leave an activity which is continuing for others, they cannot always tidy up after themselves as the materials are still in use. Should the last person in the home area or the block area have to tidy up for everyone else who used the materials? In order for children to feel responsible for the organisation of the environment, their suggestions should be tried out and evaluated by them, with adult guidance, and if necessary modified by agreement. When children become involved in this way, they see the reasons behind management procedures and want to help to make them work.

Clothing

We need to check whether children could do much more for themselves than they realise. In one of the nurseries I visit, children are expected to turn to each other for help with coats, shoes and such, using adults only as a last resort. Parents can also help by coaching children in dressing and undressing themselves rather than doing this for them. In the case of protective clothing, you may need to adapt what you have so that it *really* protects *and* can be used independently or with the help of another child. Don't be shy about demonstrating how to do this. There is little point in leaving children to 'discover' it for themselves. They may not be trying to.

Apprenticeship

Activities like paint mixing and dough making can be a task shared by adults and children working from recipe cards made up of words and pictures. Children also delight in helping to wash up with an adult or friend and this adds to what they can learn about materials and people. Eventually the children can take over these tasks. We need to make visible as much of our work as possible, rather than doing jobs out of sight. Children need to see those skilled performances discussed in Chapter 9. They need to know how their world is run and to take a hand in running it.

Movement and noise

When children are expected to collaborate and make creative use of physical resources, there will be more noise and moving around than when everyone sits and listens to the teacher. We need to look at noise levels to discover what is unavoidable and legitimate and concentrate our attack on the avoidable and reducible.

We need to discover the sources of disturbance. Where are the 'pathways'? Do they lead *to* or *through* activity areas? Are there areas of 'dead space' which lead to nowhere, suggest nothing and become places for milling about? Is there scope for privacy and cosiness as well as communal spaces? Can you see into all the areas without having to physically be here, there and everywhere? Can the children?

Learning from children

An interesting experiment was carried out involving nursery school children in the re-organisation of their classroom (Pfluger and Zola, 1974). The equipment from the classroom was removed to the school hall. The children were then allowed to fetch stuff from the hall to use in the classroom as they wished. After several weeks, everything but the piano, tables and chairs had been returned to the classroom. All the large equipment was arranged around the walls, leaving a large space in the middle, which became the general play-work-snacktime space to which all materials were brought when needed. Most in use were blocks, trucks and home-play equipment, with much mixing and matching to create complex dramatic settings.

• Is there anything we can learn from this child's-eye-view of a good play–work environment?

• Are there any aspects of this that trouble you?

MIXING AND MATCHING

Depending on how you organise your spaces and pathways, you may encourage mixing and matching or prevent it. If you don't want sand and water to be combined, don't put them next to each other, or link them via pathways.

When the dough is turned to slime by introducing it to water, it is often the result of someone's 'wonderful idea' (Duckworth, 1987). Someone thought to themselves: 'I wonder what would happen if . . . ?'. This means they saw beyond the present state of affairs to the possibility of something different, but were not sure what. It takes imagination to wonder and courage to go beyond merely saying 'what if' to checking it out. Wonderful ideas are also about transformation as when plastic bowls are transformed into microwave ovens and beads into pizzas. In principle mixing and matching materials from different areas extends children's learning because it extends the materials. In practice it can be a management headache. It is advisable to work out what is not negotiable in the way of combining stuff and shifting it around. If we can discover the children's underlying purposes, it is often possible to offer them legitimate alternatives for their experiments.

Mixing and matching extends materials thereby extending the possibilities for learning

OUT OF DOORS

The outdoor space is sometimes referred to as 'another classroom'. This is to raise awareness of the importance of opportunities for children to be outdoors in more than a milling about or recreational capacity. Although respecting the reasons, the idea of outdoors as a classroom makes me uneasy. The outside offers *unique* opportunities for being with others and learning. We need to re-discover for ourselves, by a re-appraisal of our outdoor spaces, what those are or could be. We may be struck by a wonderful idea or two.

A survey of the kind described in the previous chapter could help in identifying issues. Observing individual children's use of the outdoor facilities over a period of days and comparing this to their choices and demeanour when indoors will also offer pointers. Discussion with colleagues to discover likes and dislikes and even hang-ups are part of the process.

The timing of access to outdoor spaces is not always under our voluntary control. Even when it is, we are sometimes very set in our ways of timing opportunities for outdoor experiences. Elinor Goldschmied and Sonia Jackson (1994) suggest a flexible approach to include very small group use with one

An architectural form is incorporated in this exploration of positions in space: under, through, the other side, around

adult on occasions, rather than the mass exodus that characterises some arrangements.

HIGH/SCOPE

The High/Scope approach gives a high profile to the management of time and space *by children*. Competence in time and space management is seen as important learning for life, not simply as a means of making life more manageable in the here and now. Consequently, time is *specifically* allocated in High/Scope classrooms for learning these skills. For example, the children are taught to approach a block of time in an orderly sequence involving first planning, then carrying out the plan, and lastly looking back at how the plan worked out. This sequence is summed up as 'plan–do–review'. The idea is to enable children from an early age to become aware that they are not entirely in the grip of circumstances; that they can and do have an influence on what happens to them and around them.

A criticism of the High/Scope approach is that it contains too many fixed routines, which may be time-consuming in themselves in non-productive ways. In making time and space procedures as visible as in High/Scope they are relatively easy to follow. This may at times lead to unreflective adoption.

REGGIO EMILIA

Reggio Emilia is a town in northern Italy which has superb educational provision for children from 0–6 years. Community and collaboration characterise relationships at every level and infuse the whole learning situation. Adults and children are seen as co-researchers. Their research projects are based on the people, places, events, beliefs, hopes and dreams which are the fabric of their lives. No time limits are set for finishing projects, which are allowed to take their course. As a project takes shape, the same ideas are visited and re-visited from many different angles, with adults and children working side-by-side, week after week. Sometimes the children take their cue from the adults and sometimes the other way round. It seems that in concentrating on depth of learning by taking longer over it, they may also achieve breadth (this is also the thinking behind the child study recommended in the previous chapter). This contrasts sharply with approaches which attempt to 'cover' a greater range of content more thinly. Every child is given the opportunity to take part in an in-depth project during the school year.

The projects are pursued both in school and out in the wider community, often in collaboration with the townsfolk. Inside the schools themselves, the physical spaces emphasise connection, meeting, transaction, communication, collaboration, light, illumination, reflection. Physical boundaries are penetrable or surmountable; walls are translucent, semi-opaque, or if solid have holes in them to admit sounds, scents and a view of the other side.

Reggio Emilia is a salutary reminder that the environment speaks. What are our environments saying?

SUMMARY

Time and space structures can make or break what we and the children set out to do. When children and adults share the responsibility for managing materials, time and space, there is a good chance that more will be attempted and achieved by all. As adults, we are freer to observe and interact with the children and they are enabled to operate intelligently and responsibly in the environment.

The structuring of space and time does not have to be as visible as in the High/Scope and Reggio Emilia approaches. These were offered as a means of heightening awareness of space and time as issues which impinge on our lives and which can be harnessed *as we choose*, in pursuit of our aims. Traditionally, less visible, open-ended structures have been found effective in meeting the need for flexibility and informality. This is fine, so long as we know that this is what we are doing and why. Both visible and invisible structures are a problem if they are not the result of reflection.

CONCLUSION

Reading through the book as a whole, the questions in my mind have been: 'What do I know about children, adults and stuff, which I didn't know when I first began working with young children? Has anything changed?'

The only thing I am certain of is that I am no longer sure I have the answers – and that worries me less and less. Certainties lead to inflexibility and reluctance to dare to ask 'what if?' It induces a mind-set which gets in the way of change and development. It was *un*certainty which led me to abandon my plans for Chapter 5: Choosing Stuff. Instead the sub-text of the whole book has been about choices: those we create for children and ourselves when we adopt an enquiry-based approach.

The greatest change for me has not been in terms of knowing more but seeing more, becoming more aware. This is the result of being repeatedly challenged to justify what I do as an early years practitioner – by getting out of the water in order to see it. Awareness has also grown through the writings of others whose work as been reflected in the book: Gwen Chesters, Joan Cass, Susan Isaacs, Brenda Crowe, Vivian Paley, Chris Athey, Geva Blenkin and Vic Kelly, Linda Pound, Tina Bruce and others who have helped me keep track as I shift from whole to parts and back again to the whole.

Awareness for me has also developed through a more genuine openness to children which helps me to see, hear, think and feel more of what they see, hear, think and feel. This makes me want to work *with* rather than *for* them.

There is no research evidence, not even in official government statistics, to indicate that the developmental approach which has informed the writing of this book, fails young children. Indeed, the latest figures suggest that problems start *after* the age of seven under the present system of education in the UK. Howard Gardner (1993) suggests that there is no need to shift from a developmental to a more academic approach until around the age of nine or ten. In the early years, children are propelled forward by their urgent desire to know and come to terms with their immediate world. As they move from early childhood, they need to grasp the symbolic languages which will take them beyond the here and now. What they lack, says Gardner is motivation, reasons *of their own* which make it worth their while to go on learning. This is the area where research is urgently needed. The imposition of academic goals on the early years will not change what happens at eight, nine and ten. It will simply bring failure forward.

A trip to Reggio Emilia in Italy during 1995 confirmed for me something I have always believed: that the conditions we strive to create for the education of our young children are an expression of our humanness.

BIBLIOGRAPHY

Athey, C. (1990) *Extending Thought in Young Children*. London: Paul Chapman.

Axeline, V. (1971) *Dibs In Search Of Self*. Harmondsworth: Pelican Books.

Bartholomew, L. and Bruce, T. (1993) *Getting to Know You*. London: Hodder and Stoughton.

Blatchford, B., Battle, S. and Mays, J. (1982) *The First Transition*. Slough: NFER-Nelson.

Blenkin, G. (1995) 'You can't treat a tot like a teen.' *Independent*, 9th March.

Blenkin, G. and Kelly, A.V. (1987) *Early Childhood Education: A Developmental Curriculum*. London: Paul Chapman.

Blenkin, G. and Kelly, A.V. (1992) *Assessment in Early Childhood Education*. London: Paul Chapman.

Bretherton, I. (ed.) (1984) *Symbolic Play: The Development of Social Understanding*. New York: Academic Press.

Brown, M. (1990) *The High/Scope Approach to the National Curriculum, 1. An Introduction*. UK: High/Scope.

Brown, M. (1991a) *The High/Scope Approach to the National Curriculum, 2. The Organisation of Space and Resources*. UK: High/Scope.

Brown, M. (1991b) *The High/Scope Approach to the National Curriculum, 3. Negotiating the Use of Time with Children*. UK: High/Scope.

Bruce, T. (1987) *Early Childhood Education*. London: Hodder and Stoughton.

Bruner, J. (1980) *Under Five in Britain*. London: Grant McIntyre.

CACE (Central Advisory Council for Education) (1967) *Children and Their Primary Schools* (the Plowden Report). London: HMSO.

Carr, M. and May, H. (1993) 'Choosing a model: reflecting on the development process of Te Whariki: national early childhood curriculum guidelines in New Zealand'. *International Journal of Early Years Education*, Volume 1, No. 3: 7–21.

Cass, J. (1975) *The Role of the Teacher in the Nursery School*. London: Batsford.

Chesters, G.E. (1943) *The Mothering of Young Children*. London: Faber and Faber.

Curtis, A. (1986) *A Curriculum for the Pre-School Child*. Slough: NFER-Nelson.

Davies, M. (1995) *Helping Children to learn Through a Movement Perspective*. London: Hodder and Stoughton.

Drummond, M.J. (1993) *Assessing Children's Learning*. London: David Fulton.

Duckworth, E. (1987) *The Having Of Wonderful Ideas*. Columbia University, New York: Teachers College Press.

Edwards, C., Gandini, L. and Forman, G. (eds) (1995) *The Hundred Languages of Children*. New Jersey: Ablex Publishing.

Edwards, L.C. and Nabors, M.L. (1993) 'The creative arts process: what it is and what it is not.' *Young Children*, Volume 48, No. 3: 77–81.

Freire, P. (1974) *Education: The Practice of Freedom.* London: Writers and Readers Publishing Cooperative.

Gardner, H. (1993) *The Unschooled Mind.* London: Fontana.

Garvey, C. (1991) (2nd edition). *Play.* London: Fontana.

Geertz, C. (1973) *The Interpretation of Cultures.* New York, Basic Books.

Gifford, S. (1995) 'Number in early childhood'. *Early Child Development and Care.* Volume 109: 95–119.

Goldschmied, E. and Jackson, S. (1994) *People Under Three: Young Children In Day Care.* London: Routledge.

Gracie, M. (1977) 'The role of play'. *Forum for the Discussion of New Trends in Education,* Volume 19, No. 3: 83–6.

Gura, P. (ed.) (1992) *Exploring Learning: Young Children and Blockplay.* London: Paul Chapman.

Hackett, G. 'Checks on Nursery Schools.' *Times Educational Supplement,* 13 December 1991, p.1.

Hazareesingh, S., Simms, K. and Anderson, P. (1989) *Educating the Whole Child.* London: Building Blocks International/Save the Children's Fund.

Hutt, J.S., Tyler, S., Hutt, C. and Christopherson, H. (1989) *Play, Exploration and Learning: A Natural History of the Preschool.* London: Routledge and Kegan Paul.

Isaacs, S. (1930) *Intellectual Growth in Young Children.* London: Routledge and Kegan Paul.

Isaacs, S. (1933) (abridged edition) *Social Development in Young Children.* London: Routledge and Kegan Paul.

Katz, L.G. (1971) 'Sentimentality in preschool teachers.' *Peabody Journal of Education,* Volume 48: 96–105.

Katz, L.G. and Chard, S.C. (1989) *Engaging Children's Minds: The Project Approach.* New Jersey: Ablex Publishing Corporation.

Lowenfeld, M. (1935) *Play in Childhood.* London: Gollancz.

Malaguzzi, L. (1995) 'History, ideas and basic philosophy', in Edwards, L.C. et al. (eds) op. cit.

Matthews, J. (1994) *Helping Children to Draw and Paint in Early Childhood.* London: Hodder and Stoughton.

McAuley, H. (1990) 'Learning structures for the young child: a review of the literature.' *Early Child Development and Care,* Volume 59: 87–124.

Nelson, K. (1986) *Event Knowledge.* Hillsdale, New Jersey: Erlbaum.

Nutbrown, C. (1994) *Threads of Thinking.* London: Paul Chapman.

Paley, V.G. (1990) *The Boy Who Would Be A Helicopter.* Cambridge, Mass.: Harvard University Press.

Paley, V.G. (1992) *You Can't Say You Can't Play.* Cambridge, Mass.: Harvard University Press.

Paley, V.G. (1995) *Kwanzaa and Me: a Teacher's Story.* Cambridge, Mass.: Harvard University Press.

Pfluger, I.W. and Zola, J.M. (1974) 'A room planned by children', in Coates, G. (ed.). *Alternative Learning Environments.* Stroudsburg, Pen.: Dowden, Hulchinson and Ross.

Piaget, J. (1951) *Play, Dreams and Imitation in Childhood.* London: Routledge and Kegan Paul.

Pound, L. (1985) *Perceptions of Nursery Practice: An Exploration of Nursery Teachers' Views of the Curriculum.* Roehampton Institute, London, unpublished M.A. dissertation, University of Surrey.

Reifel, S. and Yeatman, J. (1993) 'From category to context: reconsidering classroom play'. *Early Childhood Research Quarterly*, Volume 8: 347–57.

Roberts, R. (1995) *Self-esteem and Successful Early Learning.* London: Hodder and Stoughton.

Roberts, V. (1971) *Playing, Living and Learning.* London: A. and C. Black.

Robson, S. (1993) ' "Best of all I like Choosing Time" Talking with children about play and work.' *Early Child Development and Care*, Volume 92: 37–51.

Sendak, M. (1970) *Where The Wild Things Are.* Harmondsworth: Penguin.

Stallibrass, A. (1974) *The Self-Respecting Child.* London: Thames and Hudson.

Sylva, K., Roy, C. and Painter, M. (1980) *Childwatching at Playgroup and Nursery School.* London: Grant McIntyre.

Taylor, P.H., Oxon, G. and Helley, B.J. (1972) *A Study of Nursery Education.* London: Evans/Methuen Education.

Wells, G. (1987) *The Meaning Makers: Children Learning Language and Using Language to Learn.* London: Hodder and Stoughton.

Whalley, M. (1994) *Learning to be Strong: Setting up a neighbourhood service for under-fives and their families.* London: Hodder and Stoughton.

Whitehead, M. (1990) *Language and Literacy in the Early Years.* London: Paul Chapman.

Whitehead, M. (1996) *The Development of Language and Literacy.* London: Hodder and Stoughton.

Wing, L.A. (1995) 'Play is not the work of the child: young children's perceptions of work and play.' *Early Childhood Education Research Quarterly*, Volume 10, No. 2: 223–47.

Yardley, A. (1970) *Sense and Sensitivity.* London: Evans Brothers.

Index